3. 5. 80

HOW YOU CAN SHARE IN THE FORTUNES BEING MADE IN GOLD

HOW YOU CAN SHARE IN THE FORTUNES BEING MADE IN GOLD

Robert Wolenik

Contemporary Books, Inc.
Chicago

Library of Congress Cataloging in Publication Data

Wolenik, Robert.
    How you can share in the fortunes being made in
gold.

    Includes index.
    1. Gold.   I. Title.
HG289.W64   1980   332.63   79-29743
ISBN 0-8092-7041-2

Copyright © 1980 by Robert Wolenik
All rights reserved
Published by Contemporary Books, Inc.
180 North Michigan Avenue, Chicago, Illinois 60601
Manufactured in the United States of America
Library of Congress Catalog Card Number: 79-29743
International Standard Book Number: 0-8092-7041-2

Published simultaneously in Canada by
Beaverbooks
953 Dillingham Road
Pickering, Ontario L1W 1Z7
Canada

Disclaimer

The reader should take special note of this disclaimer. The purpose of this book is to report on how individuals are making profits in gold. However, no one can predict the future nor account for luck and no assurance or guarantee is given that you will have a successful investment if you follow any of the methods, strategies, or material in this book. None of the material in this book should be construed as an investment recommendation nor should you rely on any material in this book. Before making any investment you should secure your own information and then first consult with your own accountant, attorney, or other financial advisor.

Contents

Preface

There's a golden revolution taking place in America.

News of gold makes the front page of every major newspaper in the country. There is talk of gold on radio and television. Investors who once speculated with eagerness and excitement in stocks are now devoted to buying and selling gold. The simple truth of the matter is that there's lots of money to be made in gold.

Does that mean that investing in gold is easy? Yes and no. It is easy in the sense that gold is readily available, in jewelry, in watches, in coins, in ingots, even occasionally in nuggets. But, not all of these are equally good investments. Some are better than others, a few are far better than others.

Then, there's the timing. The price of gold has not gone steadily upward throughout history as some contend. The price has gone up *and* down. During the past five years the price has spent almost as much time going down as it has spent going up.

Of course, it is the dramatic highs which capture all the attention, as when gold broke the "magic" barrier of $300 an ounce, then, almost immediately, shot up past $400.

But, such rapid appreciation is rare. It is the shrewd investor who buys when gold is low and then sells when it is high who makes the profits. (As we'll see in Chapter 6, it is also possible to make a profit when gold drops in value.) Half of making a profit in gold is knowing what to buy. The other half is knowing when to buy. We'll cover both halves in this book.

The purpose of this book is to bring the sometimes mysterious world of gold out into the open for both the brand new investor as well as the investor who would like to sharpen his techniques. It will explain what's happened to gold in the past and what's likely to happen in the future. It will explain how the price of gold is determined, where gold comes from and who buys it. It will make clear such terms as "good delivery bar," and "fineness," "bullion," and dozens of others. Finally, it will explain why I think gold, if wisely purchased, will make a good investment for the future.

If you've been sitting on the sidelines watching all those people make their fortunes in gold, this book will offer you the opportunity to join in. It will give you your chance in gold.

Introduction: Why buy gold?

Why buy gold? The simple reason that many readers of this book might give is profit. Others have made fortunes in the gold market and now you too want to join in. This is a perfectly reasonable motive. However, it may not be the only one you have. We've all heard about gold our entire lives and down deep some of the things we've heard and come to believe could affect our investment decisions. In order to be a successful investor it is important to know exactly why you are making a particular purchase.

While there are many individual reasons for buying gold, there tend to be four which have historically been central to gold purchase. People buy gold because it is beautiful; people buy gold because it is a financial hedge against an economic collapse; people buy gold for its mystique; finally they buy gold as an investment. Let's briefly examine each.

Golden beauty

Gold has many unusual properties besides just being a soft yellow metal. In printing, gold is one of the hardest colors to reproduce, silver being a close second. (One solution some expensive print jobs have used is to actually put small quantities of gold in the ink.) Gold is extremely malleable, which simply means that it can be hammered flat into very thin shapes. With gold it is possible to put a film on glass or other suitable material that is only a few molecules thick. One ounce of gold can be flattened to the point where it could cover the roof and walls of a moderate sized home with an unbroken film.

Gold is also durable. It does not get used up in the way that other materials do. It is possible, even likely that much of the gold of the ancient world, melted down, today resides in the vaults of banks across the world.

Finally, gold is precious. There is relatively little of it compared to other metals. It has been said that if all of the gold ever mined were to be placed in a single giant cube, it probably would only measure about 18 yards on a side.

These qualities contribute to gold's desirability and to its beauty. In ancient Egypt the finest pieces of art were created out of gold. The Pharaoh's sarcophagus was, when possible, made from pure gold. In medieval times gold was thought to be the metal of kings. The "divine rule of kings" worked its way down to gold which was thought to have restorative and healing powers. The royalty of the middle ages occasionally sprinkled gold on their food (much as we sprinkle salt and pepper) to reaffirm their royal status and to keep them youthful. Even today in certain restaurants in Paris and New York it is possible to buy a cake with real gold foil decoratively placed on top. (The ingestion of gold can, by the way, be hazardous to your health.)

In modern times those who buy gold for beauty primarily buy jewelry and watches. (Although, those who buy gold coins with numismatic or collector value can also be said to be purchasing for appearance.)

Up until the recent investment interest in gold, jewelry and watches accounted for about 80 percent of all gold purchases. Those who buy golden jewelry and watches for the sake of beauty, make a wise choice. Gold, as the ages have shown, is one of the most beautiful possessions an individual can have. However, those who buy jewelry as a golden investment may be ill advised.

To understand why gold jewelry is not usually considered a good investment, let's take the case of a friend of mine, Harriet, who wanted to both buy gold for its beauty and as an investment. She did so by purchasing a 12-karat gold bracelet.

We'll go into the word "karat" and what it means to jewelry in just a moment, but for now, let's just understand that when she made her purchase, Harriet was assured by the retailer that the bracelet contained exactly one ounce of pure gold. Harriet paid $400 for the bracelet. She was proud of her "investment" and wore it frequently.

About a year after her purchase, Harriet heard that the price of gold had gone up 50 percent. Since she was then in need of some cash, she decided to sell her bracelet. Since she had bought at $400, she anticipated being able to sell for 50 percent more or $600. She already had in mind what she would do with her $200 profit.

You can imagine her surprise when upon trying to resell her bracelet she was offered only $300. A $100 loss at the same time gold had gone up 50 percent in value. How could it be, poor Harriet asked?

The gold dealer who offered to buy her bracelet gave her this explanation. When she bought her bracelet the price of gold was $200 an ounce. When she sold the p' ice had gone up 50 percent or to $300 an ounce. Since her bracelet contained exactly one ounce of gold, the dealer offered her the going price—$300.

But, Harriet exclaimed that she had paid $400 for her bracelet. Since the price of gold at the time she had bought was only $200, had the retailer she bought from cheated her out of $200?

Not at all, the gold dealer said. He explained that dealers strictly in gold, such as he was, often calculate the value of their product differently from jewelry retailers. Gold dealers usually buy gold just for the metal content. They don't care what form the gold is in, whether it's a bar, a coin, or a bracelet. They're only interested in the simple metal or "bullion" value.

Jewelry, on the other hand, is more than simple bullion—it is crafted gold. In order to make her bracelet, a skilled craftsman had to work on it. The craftsman had to be paid. "Let's just assume that his fee was $85," the gold dealer said.

He then went on to explain that the retailer who sold her the gold also had to tack on his costs of operation and his profit. Jewelry retailers frequently charge as much as 50 percent of retail price on many items they carry. (If they buy for $250, they may sell for $500.) But, since gold is very competitive, Harriet's retailer, the gold dealer surmised, may have only charged about 30 percent or $115. That could be how she got to a price of $400.

Value of gold in bracelet when purchased	$200
Estimated craftsman's fee	85
Estimated retailer's mark-up	115
Price Harriet paid	$400

"The trouble," the gold dealer explained, "comes when you try to sell. I'll only buy for the gold value. In your case the price of gold would have to double before I could pay even just what you bought your bracelet for."

The gold dealer pointed out that, of course, Harriet's bracelet was lovely, a work of art, and if she could find someone who was looking to buy bracelets for their artistic value, then perhaps she could indeed sell at a profit. But, since Harriet only had one bracelet to sell (wasn't a dealer), it might be hard for her to find someone to sell to. "Even your retailer might offer a little more than I could," the gold dealer explained, "if he happened to want to buy back that kind of bracelet. But, I doubt he would offer you more than wholesale, which is still probably less than you paid for it."

The story of Harriet underlies the basic problem with buying gold jewelry for more than its beauty sake. You usually pay far more than the value of the gold content when you buy and, because you're not a dealer, have trouble selling at a similar mark-up. Usually, but not always, as we'll see in a moment.

Let's return now to the word, "karat." Gold jewelry is almost always stamped with its "fineness." Fineness simply means the quantity of pure gold in relation to the total content. In jewelry the "carat" scale has evolved. (Note: the word "karat" with a *k* refers to the fineness of gold. The word "carat" with a *c*, however, refers to a different scale, one used to measure the weight of precious stones such as diamonds in which a carat is equal to 200 milligrams. Occasionally they are interchanged by writers, but no harm is done as long as the reader understands which scale is being referred to.) This simply means that the fineness or purity of gold is expressed in karats. If a jewelry item were 100 percent pure gold, it would be 24 karats. If it were 50 percent gold it would be 12 karats. Ten-karat jewelry is actually only about 42 percent gold while 14-karat jewelry is a little less than 60 percent pure. When jewelry is less than 24 karats, which it almost always is since pure gold is too soft to withstand much handling, it is alloyed with other metal. Silver, palladium, copper, and nickel are the most commonly used alloys and, depending on which is used, give the gold its color. Silver, for example, tends to make the gold white while copper to make it red.

Harriet bought a bracelet that was 12 karat or 50 percent pure gold at a time when gold was selling for $200 an ounce. She did not make a good investment because she paid $400, far more than the going price for gold. On the other hand, if she had still paid $400, but instead bought a bracelet of 22 karat or .916⅔ fine, she would have made a much better investment. (Of course, if she had been able to buy the 12 karat, 2 ounce, bracelet for just over $200, then the current price of gold per single ounce, it too could have been a much better investment.)

In the case of 22-karat jewelry bought at very close to the

bullion value of gold, most of the purchase price would have gone to the gold, very little to the craftsmanship or the retail mark-up. Some coin dealers, currency exchangers, and other outlets do offer 22-karat gold jewelry at close to the price of gold.

If Harriet could have bought jewelry at closer to the bullion value of gold, she could have had her cake and eaten it too. She could have had both a beautiful possession *and* a good investment. Therefore, when buying jewelry for an investment as well as beauty, try to buy as close to the bullion price as possible. Of course, if you're buying for beauty alone, then you don't really care that much about gold content.

A hedge against disaster

Some people buy gold for a reason totally different than beauty. They could care less what the gold looks like, what form or shape it takes. They are buying gold the same way that a person being attacked during wartime buys a gun and ammunition. They are buying gold to stave off starvation and enslavement.

While at first glance such a person may seem to be on the "lunatic fringe," a closer examination reveals some very sane arguments. In America today we've become accustomed to a lifestyle that, for most, includes ample food, shelter, clothing, recreation, entertainment, and so forth. Most of us complain that we're not getting enough of the "good life," not that we're starving or without a shirt on our backs or a house to live in. But our world is fragile. We are, for example, dependent on a thin line of tankers carrying oil from around the world to keep our country going economically. A war in the Mideast that cuts off supplies of oil for just a single year could, as a recent Secretary of Energy put it, ". . . end the industrial world as we know it."

Most of us simply say that we can't live our lives worrying about such things. If it happens, it happens. But, some people feel differently. They feel that one should be prepared for all eventualities. Economic chaos is a real possibility, so they prepare for it.

Preparations for some can take the form of storing a year's worth of food. Most such people, however, also include buying some gold.

Why gold? Historically gold has tended to retain its value even in hard times. After the First World War, when currency in Germany became so debased that it took as many as 15 million marks to buy a single loaf of bread, gold retained value. In France of the Second World War during the Nazi invasion, French paper money was worthless. But gold coins hidden behind the moldings of doors and windows bought food and, sometimes, freedom for many families. Today as much as 5 percent of the free world's gold supply is kept hidden away in coins by French families preparing for the worst.

Even today, the survival kits for soldiers who fly missions over or infiltrate hostile territory usually contains several gold coins. Why? Because a life might be bargained for with gold, but not with paper.

What all this is hinting at, of course, is that nearly everyone knows that if the worst comes to pass—if there is depression or terrible inflation—gold will probably be the last money to retain its value. Gold was used long before paper money came into existence. And when paper money is gone, it will be used once again. Gold is the money of last resort. And that is why it is not unreasonable to put at least a small percentage of total savings into the form of gold.

The golden mystique

Gold is also bought for its mystique. Gold is frequently spoken of as a "mysterious" metal. Some believe it has mystical powers. Altars made of gold as well as images of various gods made of gold are known in most cultures, including 20th-century America. Many people wear gold wedding bands as if the metal in the bands will somehow bond the marriage just a little bit more. These applications of gold and other similar ones have one thing in common: They make use of the idea that gold has intrinsic value.

Gold has *no* intrinsic value, none whatsoever.

Gold derives its mysterious, mystical aura from a lack of understanding. The value of gold comes not from something within the gold, but from something without. It comes from the fact that people are willing to consider it valuable. Gold is like our U.S. currency (although many "gold bugs" might certainly not agree with me here).

Why does anyone accept dollars in payment for products or services? Many people believe it is because the dollar is backed by the U.S. government (and they are troubled by the fact that today the dollar has no silver or gold backing).

The real reason paper U.S. currency is so widely accepted is quite simple. We accept dollars because we know that when we, in turn, want to buy something, other sellers will accept them from us. We don't really care in the least whether the government backs up the currency or whether it's backed up with gold or silver or anything else. What we care about is that when we go down to the local store, our dollars are readily accepted for whatever we want to buy. (This is the reason that inflation is so frustrating. When we go to the store and want to buy something with dollars, we are told they won't buy as much as we think they should. In a sense the store owner is refusing to accept our money. We'll get into the economics of currency and gold more in Chapter 3.)

The proof of this can be seen during the Civil War period. The North issued "green backed dollars," paper currency fully backed by pledges of the U.S. government. No one would accept them. (Although during this period gold and silver coinage still retained value.)

The reader at this point may be a bit puzzled. We were just speaking of gold as the money of last resort. We said that even though there was economic collapse, gold retained its value. Now, it appears that we are suggesting that there may be times when even gold has no value.

That's quite true. Gold has no value when, just as with paper money, no one is willing to accept it. If our industrial world collapses and we return to a more primitive type of society such as existed during the middle ages, perhaps gold will be valued. But it takes a society to value gold. Let's consider another more terrible, but today equally real, possibility—a nuclear war.

If there were total social collapse, such as might happen during and after a nuclear holocaust, it would be the person who had food who would have something of value. When you are starving, you can't eat gold. And if no one will sell something to eat for gold (because food is very scarce and they want it for themselves), gold will be thrown away in the streets like pebbles.

This is not to suggest that gold is likely to become worthless soon, only that its value, as for all other types of money, depends on what someone is willing to give for it. Mankind has lived for many thousands of years more in a world of barter than as a money society. And, if there were to be total social collapse, you can be sure that once again barter would prevail. (It is interesting to note that the first money in the western world was struck in coinage only 2600 years ago in ancient Lydia—this is a very short time, historically speaking.)

All of this is to say that gold has no more intrinsic value than any other money. If people refuse to accept dollars, they are worthless. If people refuse to accept gold as a currency, such as might happen in times of complete collapse, then gold is no more valuable than granite.

Yet, there are some purchasers who buy gold for its mystique. They buy charms and amulets to wear around their necks and wrists. As we noted earlier, they buy rings and create golden altars. I have no quarrel with these people; in fact, I wear a gold wedding band myself. The great danger lies, however, in bringing the mystique of gold into the arena of the investment.

Gold as an investment

Lastly there are those who buy gold strictly as an investment. They have, or at least should have, one goal in mind—to make a profit. The successful investor does not cloud his or her mind with confusing goals. The investor puts aside the goals of buying gold for beauty, for a hedge against chaos and, most importantly, for its mystique.

I emphasize mystique because I believe it causes the classic error that most new gold investors make—holding onto their gold for too long.

Let's suppose that you purchased gold when the price was $300. Suddenly it spurts up to $440. Your analysis of the market and your instincts tell you it's too high. It has to fall. If you sell now and it falls to, say $400, you can buy back what you sold and show a profit of $40 an ounce. (If you're involved with 10 ounces, that's probably a very quick profit of $400.) But, I've seen too many investors who haven't cleared the mystique of gold out of their minds. Deep down, they still feel that gold's value is intrinsic, not external. They see something arcane, predetermined in the price rise. In a sense the gold is controlling the investor and not the other way around. This investor doesn't sell at $440 not believing, against his or her own analysis and instincts, that it will fall. When gold does fall (assuming our investor's market judgment was correct), our gold buyer has lost the opportunity to make a handsome profit.

There is nothing sacrosanct about gold. Investing in it is no more or less glamorous than investing in plywood, oranges, or soy beans. Those who invest in it successfully do so at arm's length, just as they would with any other investment. They make market decisions on their best judgment and on their instincts and then act upon them. They are not fooled by gold's mystique, allured by its beauty, or confused by its value as a hedge against hard times.

These are the reasons that people buy gold. For the remainder of this book we shall concentrate strictly on gold as an investment. Before we do, however, a few words should be said about investing in general.

Making an investment of any kind takes a certain amount of character. It has been said before, but bears repeating, that the only difference between an investment and gambling in Las Vegas is on whose table you place your bet. Investment involves risk. However, good investors, those who tend to come away winners in the long run, spend a great deal of time studying their investments. They learn all they can about what they are buying and selling in the hopes that they can narrow the odds against them. Just as in gambling, there are no sure bets in investments. But, careful planning and good judgment can reduce the risks.

This book is intended as an introduction to gold investment. It will give you background, analysis, and facts. But, it is not the final word. The gold market may have changed by the time you read this book. New highs may have been reached, or the price may have tumbled. New factors may be influencing the supply or the demand of gold. If you are to be a successful investor, you must not stop your research here. You should read every book on gold you can find. At the end of several chapters I've listed a number of books and periodicals which can help you get up-to-date information. You should talk with gold dealers and, if possible, with those who have already successfully invested in gold. They can give you a feel for the current market. Above all else, before you invest in gold or anything else, check with your own accountant or attorney.

1

How to make a gold investment

The first thing everyone wants to learn, understandably, is, "How do I make a profit?" Making a profit in gold can be easy when the market is shooting up. You just go out and buy some gold, wait until the price goes up, and then sell it back for more than you paid. For example, you buy gold at $300 an ounce, wait until it goes to $375 an ounce and sell back. The difference between what you paid and what you sold for, $75 an ounce, is your profit. If you bought 10 ounces, your profit is $750; 100 ounces—$7,500; 1,000 ounces—$75,000; and so on. The greater your investment, when the price goes up, the greater your profit. Of course, if you buy at $300 an ounce and the price drops to $225, you have a loss of $75 an ounce, $750 for 10 ounces, $7,500 for 100 ounces, and so on, *if you sell*. Therefore, unless you're playing the commodities futures market, which we'll discuss in Chapter 6, by buying the actual gold you can only make a profit when it goes up in price.

Almost too simple-minded to mention? Perhaps, yet between

the buying and the selling there are a lot of pitfalls that can cost you the profit you anticipated making. To begin with, where does one buy gold?

Gold in one form or another is sold for investment at banks, at currency exchangers, and at coin dealers around the country. The biggest sellers of small, individual lots of gold are undoubtedly the coin dealers.

It may come as a surprise to many readers to hear that coin dealers are big in gold. Many of us have the image of a coin dealer as being a very small business person with a tiny store often tucked away in the back of a shopping center. Such an image sees the dealer catering to a small, select group of "numismatists" or coin collectors. Nothing could be further from the truth.

Today there are major coin dealers in every large city and they are big business. One dealer in Los Angeles does over $100 million annually in sales! Several others around the country sell more. Coin dealers today often own large buildings which are filled with both gold and rare coins. (Like gold, rare coins have boomed in value with several of the rarest selling in the half-million-dollars-apiece range.)

There is a very good reason why coin dealers sell gold and it has to do with the marketability of the precious metal. To understand this point, let's go back to my friend Harriet who we met in the last chapter.

You'll recall that Harriet had some problems with a bracelet. After her bracelet episode, a friend who had heard about her troubles told her that he had some gold he was willing to sell. It was a small bar of gold weighing just three ounces that he had inherited from his father years earlier. Apparently it had been mined in the U.S. in the 1920s and then refined and formed into a bar. He was willing to sell for the going rate of gold, which Harriet knew quite well was then $300 an ounce. She bought the gold for $900.

A few months later the price of gold jumped to $350 an ounce. Now, Harriet thought, is the chance to recoup some of the losses on the bracelet. She took the gold bar to the gold dealer and demanded $1,050 ($350 times 3 ounces). The dealer looked at her sadly and said that he was very sorry, but he couldn't even give her 10 cents for the gold bar, at least not until it was "assayed." Again Harriet was shocked and asked what he meant. He explained that an "assay" is simply a chemical analysis of the gold to determine its purity. Did the bar contain three ounces of pure gold? If it did, then the value was indeed $1,050. But, what if it contained only 90 percent pure gold with the remaining 10 percent being of a base metal, such as copper? Then it was worth only 90 percent of $1,050 or $945.

Harriet said to do the assay. Again the dealer smiled sadly. He explained that he didn't do assays himself, only special firms did them and they were fairly expensive, perhaps a hundred dollars or more. Harriet exclaimed that the cost of the assay could eat up all the profit she had hoped to make on the bar and more. The dealer nodded.

Harriet's problem underscores another concern with gold investment. First she learned that in order to be able to resell at a profit, she had to buy at or close to the price of gold. Now, she learned that in order to resell, she had to have a way of readily identifying the amount of pure gold in what she was selling.

Harriet asked suspiciously how come the dealer didn't ask for an assay when she brought in the gold bracelet earlier?

The dealer explained that the "fineness" or quantity of pure gold in relation to the total content was stamped on the bracelet—it said 12 karat or 50 percent pure gold. Nothing was stamped on the bar. But, even if there had been a fineness stamped on it, if he didn't know the manufacturer, he would still have had to insist on an assay. (The penalties for falsifying the "karat" on jewelry are severe and reputable dealers wouldn't risk them by selling mislabeled merchandise.)

Is there anything she could have purchased which could have been quickly and easily resold at or close to the price of gold, Harriet asked the dealer in desperation. He suggested a bullion coin.

Bullion coins

The word "bullion" refers to precious metal in its primary finished form. When it comes out of the ground, gold is in the form of nuggets or grains or even dust. Once it has been refined, it takes the form of bars or ingots. These ingots are "bullion."

The price of bullion gold is usually considered the lowest price for which you can purchase the refined metal. Nothing has been added to the price of the metal for crafting it into jewelry or for making it into other shapes such as coins. It is basic gold and the cost is the basic price of gold.

The price of gold bullion is set twice daily in London for reasons we shall see in the next chapter. This price is recognized around the world. A smart investor usually would try to buy as close to this price as possible.

Buying for exactly the bullion price of gold might be very difficult for most investors, however, since it is normally available at that price only in approximately 400-ounce bars! At $400 an ounce that would mean that the minimum purchase price would be $160,000!

Help is at hand, however, for the small investor. Dozens of nations regularly issue or have issued gold coins that are sold close to the bullion price of gold. Since they are struck by government or large private mints, they are easily recognized. This means that you can buy these gold coins at close to the bullion price for gold and not have much trouble in reselling them (no assay usually required). Several large banks, mainly Swiss, also strike easily recognized ingots or small, usually 1 ounce, bars.

There are over 100 bullion coins that are available and many are listed in Chapter 8. Also listed are their gold content, their size, and distinguishing characteristics, as well as some of the reasons they may be popular or unpopular with collectors.

There are, however, eight gold bullion coins which are the most popular either because of their availability, their size, or the fineness of the gold within them.

(Note: You'll recall that in the introduction we were speaking of the quantity of gold or "fineness" as expressed in karats in jewelry. In bullion gold, fineness is expressed as a decimal. A bar, for example, might be stamped, ".916⅔ fine." This would mean that the bar contains 91.6⅔ percent gold with the remainder being some base metal.)

Gold in bullion coins is also expressed in fineness which is given for each coin in Chapter 8. For our purposes, however, we'll consider the eight most popular bullion coins just giving the direct amount of gold in each (how many ounces of gold each contains). The coins are:

Coin	Approx. gold content	Source
Krugerrand	1 ounce	South Africa
Maple Leaf	1 ounce	Canada
Franklin	1, ¼, ½ ounce	private United States
50 peso	1.2 ounces	Mexico
Sovereign	.2354 ounces	Great Britain
100 corona	.98 ounce	Austria/Hungary
4 ducat	.444 ounce	Austria
1 ducat	.111 ounce	Austria

All of these coins sell at a small premium above the bullion price of gold. We'll discuss the premium in just a moment, but first, let's consider each coin. (Note: A more complete description of the coins can be found in Chapter 8.)

Krugerrand

The Krugerrand is the most popular bullion coin. Until recently it accounted for about 70 percent of U.S. sales and about 80 percent of small gold sales in Europe. Unlike most other coins it has no denomination stamped on it. (The denomination is the "face value" or what the government says it is worth. The U.S. dollars say "one dollar" on the face, the dime says "one dime," and so forth.) Rather, the Krugerrand has stamped on it "one ounce of pure gold." In actuality, however, the Krugerrand weighs more than an ounce. It is .916⅔ fine or about 92 percent pure gold. The coin has about 8 percent base metal, so its gross weight must be over an ounce to net 1 full ounce of gold.

The advantage of the Krugerrand is the ease in determining its price. Since it contains 1 ounce of gold, its price is simply the bullion price of gold *plus* a small premium. If gold is selling for $200 an ounce, the price of the Krugerrand is $200 plus the premium. If gold is $400 an ounce, the Krugerrand is $400 plus the premium.

The reader should understand, of course, that it is important to know the *current* price of gold. Recently, gold has fluctuated as much as $20 an ounce over just a few hours. It is vital to know the last London fixing, but this is easy to find. Virtually all dealers post the London price of gold. Also it is broadcast daily on many radio and television stations. Newspapers usually give *yesterday's* gold prices, so be careful with that source.

Premium

We mentioned that the Krugerrand sells for the bullion price of gold plus a small premium. Just what is that premium? The premium is a fee that is paid for the privilege of not having to buy gold in a 400-ounce bar. It is usually quite small, around 3 to 4 percent for the Krugerrand. It includes the following expenses:

> Cost of minting
> Cost of transportation
> Insurance
> Distributor's costs and profit
> Retailer's costs and profit

One would think that these expenses would add heavily to the cost of the coin. Yet, usually they don't amount to more than 4 percent. For example, when the bullion price for gold is $300, the retail selling price of the Krugerrand may be around $312 to $315. The price you have to pay a dealer to purchase the coin is only about $12 to $15 dollars more than the bullion price. It is a small price to pay for the convenience.

One question that may arise in some readers' minds is, Why is there a $3 variation? Why isn't it simply $312, in our example? Why is it $312 to $315?

The answer for the price variation has to do with the availability of the Krugerrand. It has to be shipped all the way from South Africa. When there is heavy demand, more buyers than sellers, there may be a temporary shortage of Krugerrands. That puts an additional premium on its sales. Instead of being sold for the normal bullion price plus normal premium, in our example, $312, the shortage of Krugerrands may boost their price up to $315 or a bit more. Of course, if the price gets much higher than that, buyers turn their attention to the other bullion coins.

One other factor affecting the premium on the Krugerrand is the direction of the gold market. If the price of gold has been rising, dealers may charge a bit more for the Krugerrand anticipating the price rise. If gold has been falling they may charge a bit less anticipating the fall.

Of course, buying is only one aspect of investing in gold. There is also selling. When an investor sells a Krugerrand back, does he or she lose the premium that was paid upon purchase?

No, not entirely. Dealers are usually able to buy new Krugerrands from the South Africa distributor at about a 2 to 3 percent mark-up. Since they sell at about a 3 to 4 percent mark-up their margin is only about 1 percent. Both their overhead and profit have to come out of this. When gold bullion is selling for $300 an ounce, that means their mark-up is only about $3 per coin. Very small indeed.

On resales, dealers usually double their mark-up. This means that when you sell they're charging you around 2 percent. Usually you can sell back a Krugerrand at 2 percent below what it is retailing for. In our example, with gold at $300 an ounce and a Krugerrand selling at $312, you probably can sell back around $306. This also applies to the additional premiums for market direction and Krugerrand scarcity. If the coin is selling retail for about $315, when the bullion price of gold is $300, you can usually sell back at about $309.

Krugerrand

Reproductions do not
represent actual size.

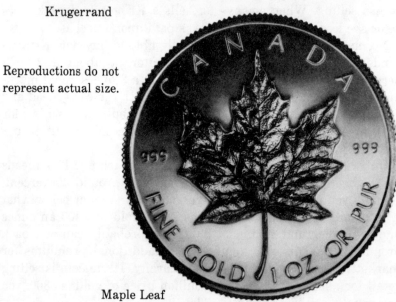

Maple Leaf

Mexican 50 Peso

Reproductions do not
represent actual size.

100 Corona

1 Ducat

Sovereign

4 Ducats

The investor's differential, or loss due to the coin's premium then, is only about 2 percent. Very small indeed.

Of course, the reader should understand that the premiums indicated here are for a steady, large market. In a market in which price is rapidly increasing or decreasing, or in a small market, the premium may vary more. Also, the premium may vary at different times and in different parts of the country. While the premium structure shown here should serve as a guide, it is best to check with local coin dealers to see what their premiums are. Most will discuss them quite openly. There are few secrets when it comes to gold.

The premium structure for the other seven most popular bullion coins tends to be similar to that for the Krugerrand. While we won't go into them in as much detail here, let's take a few moments to consider some of their more significant investment characteristics.

Maple leaf

This coin was first issued by Canada in mid-1979 as a direct competitor to the Krugerrand. Many experts feel that because it originates just across our northern border, once distribution gets fully established it may have a smaller premium than the Krugerrand and may supplant it in popularity in the U.S.

Franklin

This is not a coin, but a medal produced by the Franklin Mint in Pennsylvania. The Franklin Mint is the world's largest private mint handling the coining needs of several foreign governments. The Franklin is their venture into the bullion coin field. The 1-ounce coin/medal has a premium close to that of the Krugerrand. However, because it is not an official coin (government issue) in some areas and in some quantity purchases it may require the payment of a sales tax that a Krugerrand might not. Check with your local dealers for details on this.

The Franklin also comes in ½- and ¼-ounce sizes. This offers the very small investor the opportunity to get into gold. A bullion price of $300 an ounce or higher may simply be too much for some investors. A coin/medal containing ¼ of an ounce will offer the opportunity to get into the field at a much smaller initial investment. The premium on these small pieces, however, seems to be running, proportionately, significantly higher than for a Krugerrand.

Peso, sovereign, and corona

These foreign bullion coins are similar to the Krugerrand. However, because they do not contain a simple 1 ounce of gold, the computation of their value is a little bit more tricky. The 50 peso, for example, contains roughly 1.2 ounces of gold. That means that when gold is selling for $300 an ounce, an investor must first multiply the bullion price by 1.2 ounces ($300 × 1.2 = $360). In this case, the price of the coin would be $360 plus the premium. For the sovereign the calculation is even more complicated ($300 × .2345 = $70.35 plus the premium).

Many buyers get confused by these odd numbers which somehow seem unrelated to the going price of gold. That probably accounts for the unpopularity of the coins. Nonetheless, they make excellent bullion pieces and, when Krugerrands are in short supply, can make good sense as an investment.

Ducats

The 4 and 1 Austrian ducats have an advantage similar to the Franklin we were just discussing. Their smaller size means that a smaller initial investment is required to get into them. In addition, the coins are nearly pure gold. Their fineness is .986⅔ or nearly 99 percent pure. This is much finer than the other coins and offers certain advantages to some users. Their higher fineness means that the coins may command an additional premium. (We'll see in the next chapter why very high fineness in gold is difficult to obtain and is of special use.)

In addition to these coins, several sources also mint ingots.

Probably the most popular is the 1-ounce ingot offered by the Swiss Credit Bank. It is rectangular in shape and states "Credit Suisse" on it. It also sells for a small premium above the bullion price of gold and because it is so easily recognized rarely requires an assay.

CHART 1A   TYPICAL GOLD COIN PREMIUMS*

Coin	Approximate premium above price of gold
Krugerrand	3–6%
Maple Leaf	10–15
Franklin	4–10
Sovereign	20
100 corona	3–4
4 ducat	6–10
1 ducat	10–15
2 peso	50
20 peso	10
50 peso	4–5

*The premiums listed here are approximations compiled by observations of the author. They are based on an active competitive market such as Los Angeles or New York. In less competitive markets the premiums will tend to be higher, sometimes much higher. In addition, these premiums may rise or fall significantly depending on whether the market is going up or going down.

Counterfeits

Anything that is valuable will cause counterfeiting. Gold coins (and ingots) are no exception. Counterfeit gold coins are struck in a variety of countries, primarily those bordering the Mediterranean Sea. Experts who have examined these counterfeits frequently say that they are very nearly the same quality as authentic coins, in a few cases even superior in design to their real cousins!

Most counterfeits are struck in imitation of numismatically valuable gold coins. We'll go into detail about numismatic gold coins in Chapter 7, but for now let's just say that the premium on these coins is very high, often 40 percent or higher. (As we'll see, this is a different kind of premium.) Buyers are willing to pay such premiums because of the rarity of such coins. It is a two factor market. One factor is the bullion value. The other factor is the rarity. Most U.S. coins such as the $20 gold piece (double eagle) or $10 gold piece (eagle) are in this category. It is easy to see why counterfeiters would tend to copy these coins— the 40 percent or higher premium is a big incentive.

Counterfeiters also, however, counterfeit bullion gold coins. With premiums so small here, they have another purpose in mind. They usually short the gold in the counterfeits. This means that the coin ends up having a lower fineness than it should.

This shorting the gold in a coin is a tricky and difficult process. You'll recall that we said earlier that it is the other material in the gold (copper, silver, palladium, etc.) that affects the color. If less gold is put into a coin, more of something else will have to take its place and the color will be changed. Color, therefore, is one indication of a false coin. (Gold, however, itself comes in several shades depending on which part of the world it was mined. It may take an expert to tell a false coin by color alone.)

One method of avoiding the color problem, counterfeiters have discovered, is to "layer" the coin. The center, which can't be seen, contains the base metal, while the outside contains normal quality gold. This usually, however, creates a problem with weight. A quick test of the coin's weight and its specific gravity (which can be performed even by an amateur with a special scale costing under $150) can usually reveal this fake.

The best assurance of a coin's authenticity, however, is to know whom you're buying it from. Reputable dealers buy their gold bullion and numismatic coins only direct from the minting source, or from other dealers, investors, and collectors whom they know. They examine their merchandise and are usually experts at spotting fakes. If you buy your gold coins from them regularly, when it comes time to sell, they will know you and will usually readily buy the coin back. There's no absolute way to avoid a counterfeit coin, but each day tens of thousands of investors buy and sell coins through their regular dealers with no problems whatsoever.

Measuring gold

Since gold is measured in ounces, new buyers looking for a convenient number to buy often consider buying a "pound." If you were to go into a dealer and ask to buy a pound of gold, you would only cause confusion. The reason has to do with the system of weights used in the U.S. In this country we use the "avoirdupois" system which has 16 ounces to the pound. It is simply the measuring system used on your bathroom scale. Gold, however, does not use the bathroom scale system of weights. It uses the troy system which is based on a pound of 12 ounces. What it all comes down to is a different weight for troy ounces than for bathroom scale ounces. When we ask for a pound (bathroom scale type) of gold, what we are really asking for is about 14.58 troy ounces.

The simplest way to avoid the confusion, however, is to never ask for a pound of gold. Gold is *always* bought and sold by the ounce whether it be a single troy ounce or 750,000 troy ounces (although very, very large quantities are measured in terms of metric tons).

A word of caution. Once you buy your gold, store it carefully. Many investors consider a safety deposit box the only acceptable place for gold coins. Leaving them around the house, particularly if you let people know you're an investor, may only be inviting theft.

2

The gold countries

The pricing of gold has evolved over a long period of time and, historically, has a surprisingly large amount to do with where the gold comes from. In order to understand how gold is priced today and why the price must be above certain levels, or costs of production, it's a good idea to take a quick look at the gold countries.

Gold is a mineral that occurs naturally all over the world. Only in a few rare places, however, does it occur in sufficient quantities to warrant mining. Those places include small areas of South America, North America, Asia, and Africa.

In the ancient past, gold came, amongst other places, from the fabled mines of King Solomon. These were probably located somewhere in northeast Africa. In the middle ages gold was mined at several small locations in Europe. But, the real beginning of big gold mining, at least as far as most Americans are concerned, came with the '49ers and the fabulous gold strike in California in the last century. (Note: Prior to the California gold strike, the precious metal was mined extensively in Georgia and other southern states. There was even an official mint in Dalonega, Georgia, to coin the metal mined nearby.)

The California gold occurred in thin veins that streaked downward throughout the earth. Where these veins broke through the surface, some of the gold would chip off and be washed away by rains. Much of this gold eventually found its way into creeks and other tributaries. In 1848 California literally had golden rivers. The first gold miners only needed a shallow pan to get their gold. Water and a bit of sand was scooped into the pan. Then the sludge was swirled around until the lighter sand flew off the sides and the heavier gold lay at the bottom. Occasionally whole nuggets were found in this manner.

Since the land was virgin territory, even the most inexperienced "city boy" could quickly pan a few grains of gold out of many of California's streams. And city dwellers did come to make their fortune. Even today there are still early photos of the scene in San Francisco Bay with hundreds and hundreds of abandoned sailing ships. Both the passengers and the crews had left the ships for the goldfields.

This type of gold found in streams had a name. It was called placer gold and they even named a town in California after it, Placerville. But, all too quickly what it had taken nature millennia to lay down was gathered up. Soon the placer gold was all gone and anyone wanting more gold had to go through the hard work of digging down into the veins in the earth for it. The free ride for gold was over.

It was about this time, in the 1850s, that the fabulous Comstock lode was found. The Comstock, located in the Sierras between California and Nevada, consisted primarily of a number of very deep *silver* mines. That's correct, silver. Since gold and silver are often found together, much gold was also produced, but far more silver. This was significant to the money in America as we'll later see.

The mining posed severe problems. Often it was necessary to go down thousands of feet. But, the Sierras were covered with snow in the winter and that snow turned to water in the spring and summer. They were mountains filled with water and the mines frequently flooded. In Jackson, in the heart of the Sierras, giant pumps were used to clear the mines. The pumps had to be enormous to suck the water out from the deep levels and coupled with already high costs of labor and materials associated with deep digging, mining became very expensive. Gold in those days was well under $20 an ounce, yet mining costs were rapidly approaching that figure. Eventually, there was no more profit in the mines and they had to close. The gold in them, however, was far from exhausted. Even to this day whenever gold makes a surge forward in price, there are new attempts to get the water out and the mines opened again.

On the western side of the Sierras, the problem was equally severe. The mine owners vowed they would give half their fortunes to any man who could solve the water problem. One man, named Sutro, did, for a time. Four thousand feet below the opening of the nearest mine, and on the California slope of the mountains, he dug a hole straight in. It was tall enough for a man and a mule to walk through. Eventually he connected up with several mines and drained their water out from the bottom!

Sutro's tunnel made him famous. With his wealth he later built a fabulous house on a cliff overlooking the Pacific Ocean in San Francisco which later opened to the public offering hot mineral baths. Even into this century it was a tourist attraction. But, the tunnel was only in operation for a few years. Frequent cave-ins were a problem. Eventually many veins petered out and the low price of gold and silver closed most of the rest.

Today in the United States there are only two or three mines in operation. Perhaps the Homestake in South Dakota was the most famous. It squeaked through the hard times. Another source of gold has been the huge Kennecott copper mine in Utah where gold is an important by-product.

Shortly after gold was discovered in California, it was also discovered halfway around the world in Australia. Suddenly, hundreds of thousands of individuals from England and else-where descended on the former penal colony to search for gold. And, like the California gold rush, the surface gold was quickly gathered up. Soon expensive deep mine operations were started up. By the turn of the century Australian mining, helped by the local government, was producing nearly 2 million ounces of gold a year. Recent production, however, has only been about a fourth of that.

In the 1890s gold was also discovered in the Yukon territory of Canada. It was freezing cold in the winter and wet in the summer, yet a whole new generation of fortune-seeking Americans pushed north. Much of the gold was found in the U.S. territory of Alaska and one of the quickest ways to get there was through White's Pass in Canada. Early photographers took pictures of the hopeful trying to cross the steep pass. The Canadian Mounties turned back everyone who could not bring a full year's supply of food with them. Dead donkeys with the broken loads of the unsuccessful strewed the path. The Klondike gold rush was short lived. At its biggest point it probably only took about a million ounces a year of gold out of the ground. And, as in Australia and California before it, big mining operations settled in to get the hard gold out and eek out small profits on large investments.

Shortly before the Klondike discovery (but not really appreciated until much later) gold was found in South Africa. Legend has it that a prospector named George Harrison was hired by a widow named Oosthuizen to dig a well. Along the way he noticed that the ground was of the sort to bear gold, and, upon closer examination, he did indeed find gold. Harrison reported his find in a letter in 1886 to Johannes Paul Kruger who was then President of the Republic.

Immediately mining commissioners were sent out to survey the area and they reported that indeed it had gold, but it was not like any that had been found elsewhere. It was dust, thinly spread throughout the earth. There would be no chance to gather in nuggets and grains as had been the case earlier in Canada and California and just a year or two later in Australia. Harrison, legend has it, later sold his claim for just $30.

The Oosthuizen farm was located just a few miles west of what is today the city of Johannesburg. Upon announcement of the discovery, prospectors and fortune seekers raced for the area. Within months thousands were there, walking over the ground and scratching their heads. The gold was there, but it would take serious mining to get it out. Those without capital left and the discovery excitement died down. Yet, the South African fields were to eventually prove to be the world's richest.

The area in which gold was found in South Africa in past geological times was probably an ancient sea. The formations in which the gold appears are known as reefs. In a few areas they reach to the surface, but in most they are underground, far underground. A shallow reef might be as little as 500 feet below the surface, a medium reef 4,000, and the deepest reefs 12,000 feet or deeper.

Discovering the mines in South Africa was not as easy as it had been in America. In the western U.S., gold outcroppings would lead prospectors to rich mines. In South Africa the closest the gold got to the surface might be a mile or more underground. In order to find mines, appropriate geological formations had to be discovered and then bore holes dug deeply into them searching for a vein.

The vein itself might be a foot or just a few inches thick, but it would spread out over a great area. In order not to miss it, samplings from each bore hole would have to be examined every few inches all the way down. It was very expensive work. And to add to the expense was the additional problem of water and heat. The first goldfields were known as the Rand fields (later West Rand). To the west of these at the turn of the century were discovered what became known as the Far West Rand Fields. Removing the gold here was virtually impossible because a sheet of dolomite nearly 4,000 feet thick and filled with water and sludge covered the reef.

It wasn't until the 1930s that a German geophysicist, Dr. Rudolph Krahmann, using a magnetometer, was able to identify the exact location of the fields. Drilling began which proceeded through layers of lava to several thin gold-bearing reefs. But, the mud and water still continued to plague deeper drilling. Finally, a technique that involved injecting cement under pressure ahead of the drill to seal the water out as drilling went down proved effective in getting to the rich gold-bearing material.

Once the reef was found there was the problem of keeping the mines open. Great pumps had to be installed to remove water and giant cooling units had to be built to lower the mine temperatures. Below 5,000 feet the temperature soared to above 100 degrees. As the miners approached the 10,000 foot level the temperatures rose to above 130 degrees.

Finally, the reef itself was like a thin wafer. Very wide, but not very thick. Miners found it impossible to remove only a foot or less of gold-bearing earth. The minimum amount that could be removed was usually a section 4 feet thick. That meant that in addition to 1 foot or less of ore-bearing earth, 3 feet of non-productive ground had to be hoisted to the surface, miles above, for refining. It was a staggering problem. (In recent years new techniques have reduced the amount of non-productive earth that has to be hauled from the mines.)

The result of all these problems was increased cost. In America it resulted in virtually closing down the gold mining industry. In Australia and Canada the industries survived at relatively low levels mainly because of government subsidies. In South Africa, however, for years the mines were operated at full capacity because plentiful native labor could be obtained cheaply. (It should be noted that in recent years as the price of gold has risen, so have the wages and the living conditions of the South African miner.)

The mines in South Africa cover a broad arc more than 150 miles wide near Johannesburg. And they seem endless. As one field appears to be exhausted, another is discovered. Besides the Rand fields (East, West, and Far West), there are also the Klerksdrop area, the Orange Free State Field, the Evander field, and several newer areas. Between them South Africa is able to produce more gold than the rest of the world combined— some 20 to 30 million ounces per year.

Before we leave the South African gold, a few words need to be mentioned about the process used to get the gold out of the

earth. Since the particles of gold are very fine, a simple sedi-
mentation process with water would not work. Even the procedure found in California which used quicksilver (found in mines
in the Santa Clara Valley and hauled to the Sierras) did not
work well enough. Rather, a process involving cyanide was used.
Nearly all the gold can be removed from the earth in this
process. When it is further chemically treated it can be made
into a maximum fineness of about .96 or 96+ percent pure. This
fineness is important as we shall see shortly.

There is one other big gold source that we have not touched
upon and that is the Russian gold. Russia is probably the world's
second largest producer of gold and her significance to the
market cannot be denied. (I say "probably" because the Russians
have refused to announce their gold production or reserve
figures since the early 1930s. Gold experts can only surmise
about Russian gold supplies based on what that country sells to
the West.)

The cost of mining Soviet gold is probably the highest in the
world. Yet, the Soviets devote great amounts of their resources to
getting the gold out. We shall see why in a few moments.

Once the Soviet gold is extracted from the ground, it is refined
using a process probably similar to that used in South Africa.
However, because the Russians have access to great quantities of
hydroelectric power in the areas of their refineries, the gold is
further refined to a nearly pure state—about .9999 fineness.
Soviet gold, therefore, has become known as the finest in the
world. Since nearly pure gold is used in some coins and since it
is of great advantage in certain other applications such as in
jewelry and other fields, the Soviet gold brings a premium when
it is sold. That premium can amount to from a few cents to a
dollar or more an ounce.

The Russians sell some of their gold in Zurich, some in
France, and some in England. Their sales are substantial,
amounting to over 400 metric tons in each of the last several
years. (There are 32,151.239 troy ounces in a metric ton. Or, to
put it differently, roughly 32 metric tons equal 1 million troy
ounces of gold.)

The reason for heavy Soviet gold sales

The Soviets sell their gold to the Western world for a very specific reason—foreign exchange. Russia does not belong to the International Monetary Fund. Russian currency, the kopeck and the ruble, are not readily exchanged in currency markets.

When a company in the U.S. wishes to buy something in France, for example, it uses U.S. dollars to buy French francs in order to make the purchase. When a company in France wishes to buy a U.S. product, the transaction takes place in the other direction. The *value* of the francs and the dollars floats up and down depending on a wide variety of factors including the economies of each country, their relative inflation, their foreign trade, and so on. (For a detailed explanation see, *Buying and Selling Currency for Profit*, Contemporary Books, Inc., Chicago.)

Russian currency, however, is not allowed to float up and down. It is blocked from doing so by the Russian government (which is why rubles are sometimes called "blocked" money). The Russians state that the ruble is worth about $1.58 U.S. It is, in the Soviet Union. In the free market, however, the ruble bounces around between $.30 and $.40 to the dollar.

As long as traders between the Soviet Union and other countries have purchases and sales that balance out, there is no problem with the Soviet rubles. Russia, however, has little to sell abroad, but wishes to buy much including high technology equipment and wheat. It offers rubles at the going exchange rate to the dollar. But, sellers, such as U.S. wheat interests, since they have little desire to buy anything in Russia, have no use for the rubles. If they tried to turn them in for dollars on the open market, they would show a loss of as much as 80 percent. Consequently, Russia can't buy its wheat and high technology equipment, unless it pays for it with something other than rubles. That something is gold. Each year the Soviet Union has sold hundreds of metric tons of gold to pay for its foreign purchases.

The need to make foreign purchases, therefore, is why the Soviets devote so much of their energies to mining gold. They simply could not survive in the world without it. It has been rumored that the mines are operated with slave labor to reduce costs. Even so, the machinery alone is costly.

Because of the use Moscow puts its gold to, it does not announce production figures. Perhaps the Russians feel that if they keep the rest of the world guessing about the amount of gold they have, it will enhance their credit and keep the gold price up. In any event, the only knowledge those in the West have of Russian gold production comes from the amount of gold the Russians sell each year to pay for foreign purchases.

Other golden countries

South America has long been a treasure house of gold. The ancient Incas in Peru mined the precious metal as did the Indians in Mexico. Today, many South American countries have small gold industries. The largest is probably in Mexico, but it is shadowed by the gold produced by Russia and South Africa. Rhodesia (Zimbabwe) and the Philippines also produce some gold.

3

The economics of gold

The economics of gold may sound like the hard chapter of the book. It's really not intended to be. Here, we're simply going to look at some of the factors that influence the price of gold. This chapter is really not any harder than simple supply and demand. It will show you why the price of gold is where it is.

Gold pricing

Let's begin by seeing who sets the price of gold.

As we've seen, South Africa produces most of the world's gold. However, the cost of extracting gold from the South African fields is expensive. The cost of developing the fields involves risking great amounts of capital without any guarantee of return. At the time of the discoveries and through the early part of this century, financing for the fields in South Africa originated in part in England. The great banking houses of London were deeply involved in the South African mining business. In fact, through the 1920s virtually all of the South African gold was shipped to London for refining.

It is not surprising, therefore, that virtually all of the gold South Africa produced was shipped to England for sale. The sale even today is conducted by the five major gold dealers in London. These are Mocatta and Goldsmid, Sharps Pixley and Co. (who were instrumental in handling sales of South African gold in the early days), Samuel Montagu and Co., Ltd., Johnson, Matthey, Ltd., and N. M. Rothschild and Sons, who also have acted as the broker for the Bank of England.

Because much of the South African gold still arrives at London first, and because of historical precedent, it is the London price for the bullion that establishes the basic world price for gold. The London market deals only in bars that weigh 400 ounces (some leeway is allowed here with bars perhaps 30 ounces heavier or lighter accepted) and that are at least .959 pure. It is no coincidence that this is the fineness, as we saw earlier, that South African gold is refined to. Gold having this weight and fineness is referred to as a "good delivery" bar and is the standard form of gold sold through the London dealers.

The London market performs the extraordinarily important function of determining the price of gold twice daily. In the morning and again in the afternoon representatives of each of the five major dealers meet in the Rothschild offices. By phone they are in contact with a worldwide network of dealers. These representatives confer with one another, bargaining back and forth, until they arrive at a price at which they are willing to buy and sell gold. That price is known as the London gold "fixing." Twice daily the London price fixing on gold is announced to the world. When you go to buy gold at a dealer, chances are that the price he or she has posted for gold is the latest London fixing. It is usually the base price for Krugerrands and other gold bullion coins. (Of course, their premiums are tacked on top.)

London, however, is not the only gold market in the world. It is not even the biggest. The biggest is undoubtedly located in Zurich, Switzerland.

The Swiss have long been known for their affinity to gold. Tiny gold ingots are produced by many Swiss banks and sold over the counter. In Switzerland, citizens regularly exchange gold at banks the way we in the United States exchange paper currency for coinage. In addition, for individuals, corporations, and even governments, Switzerland is a popular place to buy and sell gold. The Swiss tend to keep very quiet about their gold business dealings. They normally will not report the identity of people who hold bank accounts (bank accounts in Switzerland can be in gold, in dollars, in Swiss francs, or other currency), but rather simply issue a number to the owner. (Swiss secrecy does not usually extend to criminal matters. However, they have been known to withhold information from other governments when the reason the information was being sought was a dispute over taxes between the account holder and his or her government.)

Because gold sales can be handled anonymously in Switzerland and because sales of gold with .959 fineness are usually not taxed there, it is easy to see why it has become the world's central gold dealer.

Since 1969, in part, most of the gold from South Africa has gone directly to Zurich avoiding the London market. If this should continue then Zurich could soon surpass London in importance. This is significant because the price of gold in Zurich is seldom the same as in London (close, but not exactly the same). The difference has largely to do with supply and demand at a particular market at a given time of the day. The Zurich market is organized by three big banks: Swiss Bank Corp., Credit Swiss, and the Union Bank of Switzerland. There are other major markets in New York and Hong Kong. While one is open, the others may be closed.

Other gold sources

What we've been looking at are the major producers and markets of *new* gold. The amount of new gold that is produced each year, however, is miniscule compared with the amount that is held in vaults and stored elsewhere. Remember, gold can be made into jewelry, melted, made back into bars, remelted, and so on indefinitely. Very likely a major percentage of all the gold ever mined in the history of the world remains with us today in one form or another.

The United States still has in its vaults a quarter of the free world's stored gold (roughly 265 million ounces). Another half of that gold is probably stored in the vaults of the major European countries, particularly Germany, France, and Switzerland. Finally, another quarter is divided among private individuals, corporations, and private banks.

Each year some of this *old* gold is brought out of vaults and sold on the open market. When the price of gold is high, more of it tends to come out. When the price is low, less of it comes out. In recent years millions of ounces have been brought out of vaults. Perhaps the largest sales have come from government bodies. Beginning in November of 1978 the U.S. began selling off gold from its reserves. Until April of 1979 it sold 1.5 million ounces a month. Thereafter it sold 750,000 ounces a month until October when it discontinued announcing in advance the date or the amounts of the sales. Since 1976 the International Monetary Fund has sold gold regularly at the rate of about ½ million ounces per month. Such sales are expected to terminate in May of 1980, however.

Total gold

Old gold sold from reserves coupled with *new* gold make up the total supply of gold each year. The chart from the Chamber of Mines of South Africa gives the history of gold supplies since 1948.

On this chart, the first column gives the combined free world production of *new* gold. This includes South Africa, Australia, Canada, U.S., and other countries. The second column lists gold supplied by the Soviet Union and other Communist countries. It can't be known what percentage of this amount is new gold and what is old. The figure, however, does represent the total amount

CHART 3A   GOLD BULLION SUPPLY AND DEMAND
1948-1978 (Metric tons)

	Free world mine production	Net trade with Communist Bloc	Total supplies	Official purchases or sales*	Net private purchases
1948	702	—	702	369	333
49	733	—	733	369	369
1950	755	—	755	288	467
51	733	—	733	235	498
52	755	—	755	205	550
53	755	67	822	404	418
54	795	67	862	595	267
55	835	67	902	591	311
56	871	133	1004	435	569
57	906	231	1137	614	523
58	933	196	1129	605	524
59	1000	266	1266	671	595
1960	1049	177	1226	262	964
61	1080	266	1346	538	808
62	1155	178	1333	329	1004
63	1204	489	1693	729	964
64	1249	400	1649	631	1018
65	1280	355	1635	196	1439
66	1285	-67	1218	-40	1258
67	1250	-5	1245	-1404	2649
68	1245	-29	1216	-620	1836
69	1252	-15	1237	90	1147
1970	1274	-3	1271	236	1035
71	1236	54	1290	-96	1386
72	1183	213	1396	151	1245
73	1121	275	1396	-6	1402
74	1006	220	1226	-20	1246
75	953	149	1102	-9	1111
76	967	412	1379	-58	1437
77	968	401	1369	-269	1638
78	969	410	1379	-362	1741

Source: Chamber of Mines of South Africa

*Definition of official sales has been extended from 1974 to include activities of government controlled investment and monetary agencies in addition to central bank operations. This category also includes IMF disposals.

brought onto the market by Communist countries each year. Free world and Communist Bloc supplies are totaled in column three. This column lists the total amount of new free world and Communist Bloc gold. For our purposes we'll consider this the total amount of *new* gold issued each year.

Skipping over to column five, we find the total amount of gold purchased each year. Since, for practical purposes, purchases today are nearly all private, this represents the total *demand* for gold.

Going back to column four we find the official purchases or sales of gold. When government agencies (including activities of government controlled investment and monetary agencies in addition to central bank operations including the IMF sales) are selling gold, the figures show a minus in front of them. When government agencies buy gold, no sign occurs in front of them. Column four represents the total supply of *old* gold placed on the market.

Column three when added to column four (new supplies plus old supplies) must equal column five. The sales equal the purchases.

Users of gold

We'll go into the supply and demand equation a bit more in a few moments, but first, let's briefly consider who buys all that gold. Private purchases consist not only of those who purchase for investment, but also those who purchase for all other reasons. Through 1978 nearly 70 percent of all the gold purchases were for jewelry and watch needs. This may be a startling figure to many who thought that the biggest portion of the market was investors.

About 16 percent of gold purchases each year go to coins, ingots, and medals. This includes the Krugerrands and other bullion coins. This is primarily an investment use.

Another 5 percent is used by electronics. Gold is one of the best conductors of electricity and is used in critical contacts on circuits. It is also used in the windshields of airplanes to change electricity into heat, which helps defogging and deicing.

About another 5 percent is used by dentistry. Gold fillings are far more common in other parts of the world than they are in the U.S. where many substitutes are used.

Finally, gold is used as a decoration on buildings, in glassware and china, and in a hundred other similar applications. This accounts for about another 4 percent of use.

Uses of gold

Jewelry and watches	70%
Coins and ingots	16
Electronics	5
Dentistry	5
Decoration	4

Supply/demand

We have seen where gold comes from and in what amounts. We have also seen where it goes. We have nearly all the elements necessary to speak about the supply/demand relationship of the precious metal. Before we do, however, let's take just a moment to speak about the nature of supply and demand itself.

The "law" of supply and demand is in reality just an observation of what takes place when people interact in a world of scarcity. (It probably should be called the law of supply, demand, and price because price is an important element.)

We do live in a world of scarcity. Of course, what comes to mind recently when scarcity is mentioned is oil. Oil is in short supply. But, in reality, everything is in short supply at one time or another—lumber, coal, even water in some arid areas. If you doubt this, consider air.

Air is normally not scarce. It is everywhere that we are. But air underwater, such as in a diver's scuba tank or in a deep mine, is scarce. In those cases, in order to get air it has to be supplied by means of a scuba tank, a compressor, or a fan. And those cost something. When air becomes scarce it is said to have an economic value—somebody is willing to pay something for it. And that leads us to "substitution."

If you want air, or, to take another example, a pair of shoes, what are you willing to pay for them? If you're willing to pay with four hours of work, then the shoes are worth four hours to you. You're substituting the work for the shoes.

Substituting hours of service for products such as shoes is an extremely inefficient way of conducting business. For one thing, getting down to fractions of hours and fractions of shoes could be tricky. For another, perhaps the shoe seller doesn't want your hours of service. He already has a helper. What he wants is bread for his table. Now, in order to get the shoes, you must go to the baker and give him so many hours of service to get the bread to pay the shoemaker. But, what if the baker already has a helper? And so forth.

What's needed is a common way of expressing value. What's needed is price.

Price can be in the form of dollars, francs, yen, gold, or silver. When it is used to establish a substitution value, it is price. (In a controlled society such as in the Communist world, price still exists. Often, however, it's determined by "quota.")

Going back to supply and demand, we can now add in price. The seller of a product naturally wants the highest possible substitution value or price for his product. The buyer naturally wants the lowest possible substitution value or price. When they both agree upon a price, a sale is made.

There is rarely, however, one sale in the world of any given product. There are usually millions. Millions of people buy orange juice, cameras, shoes, and gold. And millions of people sell these items. In the case of gold, there is worldwide knowledge of the transactions. What this means is that the price depends on how strongly the total number of buyers want gold and how willing the total number of sellers are to sell.

The supply/demand of gold

Let's assume that the supply and demand for gold is steady.

We'll say that through past transactions a price of $200 an ounce has been established as one at which both buyers and sellers are willing to freely transfer gold. That is the stable price.

Now, let's say that suddenly the demand increases. Very quickly all the gold available at $200 an ounce is purchased. But, because the demand is strong, there are still buyers who want gold. There is none left at $200 an ounce. Those demanding the gold now raise the price they'll pay. They offer $201.

A few people who had gold, who were not willing to sell at $200, now reconsider. They feel that $201 is a fair substitution value. They sell at $201. But, there is still far less gold available than the demand wants. Those who want more gold raise the price they are willing to pay to $202. A few more sellers come into the market.

Those who demand gold continue raising their price, perhaps to $210 or even $220 until enough sellers are induced to come into the market to fully meet the demand or the price goes so high that those demanding gold reconsider and decide to buy something else. We'll say that the demand is fully met at $222. At that price, gold stops increasing in price. For a moment it is in equilibrium with both buyers and sellers willing to pay that substitution value. (Note: Essentially this is what is done at the London price fixing each working day.)

Of course, gold can go up in price for another reason. It can go up if the supply goes down. In that case, the amount of gold available at, for example, $200 an ounce is suddenly reduced. Prior to the shortage, all the buyers at $200 were satisfied. Now, several can't get the gold they want. In order to get it, they begin bidding the price up.

Similarly, the price of gold can go down if either the demand decreases or the supply increases.

This, then, is what is meant by supply and demand for gold.

Before we apply supply/demand to the real world of gold, a few interesting observations should be made. Note that as the price goes up, more and more sellers are inclined to put more and more gold onto the market. What this means is that when the price of gold suddenly shoots up by $20 or more an ounce, it's bound to soon level off and even drop. As more and more sellers are induced to sell at the high prices, they eventually put more gold on the market than the demand can meet. The price topples until it reaches a new equilibrium.

The same is true as sellers begin dumping gold. As the price gets lower, more and more buyers are inclined to purchase. Eventually, the demand overwhelms the supply and the price bounces back. This accounts for the rough sawtooth appearance of the price of gold on a graph.

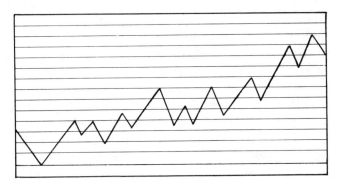

Responding to supply and demand, gold is constantly moving up and down in price trying to find equilibrium (which it can only find momentarily because there are new buyers and sellers, new demand and supply, each day on the market).

Gold in the real world

Now, let's apply supply/demand to actual gold. First the supply side of the equation. Supply is affected primarily by four sources. They are:

South Africa (new gold)
Russia (new gold for practical purposes)
Western government reserves (old gold)*
Investor sales (old gold)

---

*This is primarily sales by the U.S. government, the I.M.F., and other smaller government sales.

If any of these four suppliers of gold dramatically increases the supply of gold, the price will fall. If any reduces the supply, the price will rise. Let's take each separately.

SOUTH AFRICA uses gold production to obtain needed foreign exchange and to keep its economy going. Gold mining is one of the country's premier industries. Consequently, South Africa sells all the gold it produces as fast as it can. South Africa cannot really increase the supply of gold. It has to work hard just to keep up with present supplies. Therefore, South Africa increasing its gold supply can be eliminated as a realistic possibility. Similarly, South Africa can't withhold gold or its own economy will suffer. South Africa, therefore, tends to be a constant and consistent supplier.

On the other hand, the African continent has been involved in racial conflicts for years. There is the possibility that at some time in the future, South Africa could become embroiled in either a civil or international war that would interrupt gold supplies. It is possible that at some time in the future South Africa, therefore, might be forced to decrease its gold supplies.

Now, let's consider RUSSIA. Russia, as we've seen, is the world's second largest producer of gold. Yet, it probably spends gold as fast as it can dig it from the ground. (There has been much speculation on the size of Russian gold reserves, but their true size as we noted in the last chapter is unknown. After the First World War Russia received about 11 million ounces from Spain for safekeeping which it has never returned. Consequently, Russia might very well have substantial reserves.) Russia sells gold depending on it's need for international credit. Some years sales are up, some down.

Whenever Russia lets her intentions be known, the price of gold is almost immediately affected. For example, in early October of 1979, the U.S. announced the sale of more than 25 million metric tons of wheat, the largest sale ever, to the Russians. Within the week surrounding the announcement, the price of gold dropped by more than $60 an ounce. Prior to that announcement, however, Russia had purchased little wheat from the West, her gold sales in early through middle 1979 were down, and the price of gold was up. Russia can have a dramatic impact on the price of gold.

WESTERN RESERVES are primarily in the central banks of the various Western nations. With the exception of the U.S. these governments have not sold much in the last five years. (Although, since they hold so much, if they did it could flood the market.) Therefore, the real question is, how much gold will the U.S. sell? The U.S. has shown a tendency, as we'll see in the next chapter, to sell off its gold reserves to undercut the price of gold. The U.S., therefore, must remain a question mark.

Finally, there are the INVESTOR sales. These are very easy to predict. As the price of gold goes up, more investors sell more gold. As the price goes down, fewer sell less gold. Investors in the past have moved with the market, rather than helped to create it.

Now, let's consider the gold buyers. These include:

Users (such as for jewelry, watches, dentistry, and electronics)
Hoarders (such as the central banks of many governments and
    many private individuals)
Investors (who speculate on the price of gold)   C881347

USERS of gold behave quite orderly. When the price goes up, they try to switch to substitute metals until it comes down again. If, however, the price remains high, they usually come back to gold in the long run. When the price drops, however, they usually don't buy more, unless they're stocking up for a future price increase. They use the gold they buy in manufacturing and they can only use so much.

HOARDERS are mainly the central banks who store most of the free world's supply of gold in their vaults. Although every country is supposedly off the gold standard, governments, particularly in Europe, hoard their gold. Occasionally, they may also buy more gold. Gold purchases by German banks was noticed in 1979 (although they may have been acting for third parties).

INVESTORS will buy gold when they think the price will rise. They speculate on the market, hoping to buy low and sell high. As the price increases rapidly, more and more investors tend to jump on board, hoping to make big profits. In recent years oil-rich individuals from the Arab states have made heavy gold purchases.

If we were to plot the influences of the various segments of the gold market and their ability to effect sudden price changes, we might have Chart 3B. The direction of price influence is shown by the arrow. The approximate amount of influence on the market is shown by the width of the arrow.

Chart 3B illustrates that the biggest cause of sudden price changes upward is probably investors, of sudden price changes downward is probably government sales. Of particular interest it should be noted that the largest producer of gold, South Africa, has the littlest influence on lowering prices although it could raise them dramatically if production fell, while the biggest purchaser of gold, the users, have the least influence on raising prices. (This really isn't so strange. Although South Africa may be a supplier, that country still wants the price to be as high as possible. On the other hand, the users, though they consume most of the world's gold, want the price to be as low as possible.) Finally, Russia, by either selling or holding back gold, exerts an enormous influence on the market price of the precious metal.

One last question on economics needs to be answered—just how big a purchase or sale is needed to influence the price of gold? If one buyer in Trenton, N.J., purchases 12 Krugerrands, does the price of gold go up, even if ever so slightly? Does it take the sale of a million ounces by the Soviet Union to have any influence on the price? In other words, just how big is the gold market?

In all honesty, it is impossible to say just what effect any given purchase or sale will have on the price of gold at any time. A great deal depends on the market's momentum. For example, in November of 1978 when the U.S. announced its first sale in years of 1.5 million ounces of gold, the price plummeted. On the other hand, during the summer of 1979, each gold sale by

CHART 3B   THE SUPPLY/DEMAND OF GOLD

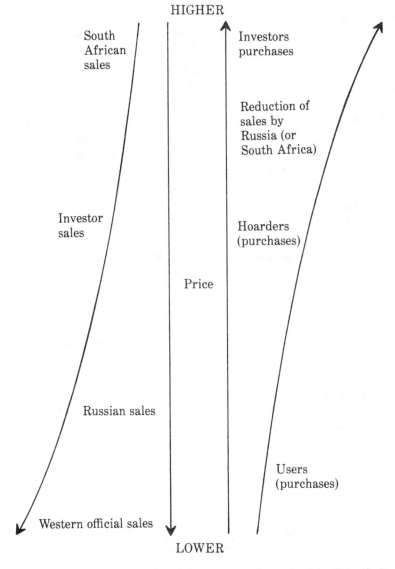

HIGHER

South
African
sales

Investors
purchases

Reduction of
sales by
Russia (or
South Africa)

Investor
sales

Hoarders
(purchases)

Price

Russian sales

Users
(purchases)

Western official sales

LOWER

The chart indicates how a particular action (purchase or sale) will be likely to affect price. It also indicates which factors have greater importance to price (widest spots between two arrows) and which have least importance (narrowest spots between two arrows).

the U.S. was followed by a sharp price increase, as much as $15 an ounce or more. In the first case, the sale scared the market by substantially increasing the supply. In the second case, the sale rallied the market when it was discovered that the demand for buying far exceeded what the U.S. was offering to sell.

In any event, the gold market is very *thin*. That means that there is little excess gold anywhere. New gold offered for sale does not meet current demand. Consider again Chart 3A.

Column one lists the total free world mine production of gold. Note that production reached a high of 1,285 metric tons in 1966. Since 1970, however, production has declined. Since 1975 it has held fairly steady, but at a rate that is roughly 300 metric tons less than production in the 1960s.

On the other hand, Russian (Communist Bloc) sales have been up, averaging over 400 metric tons a year since 1976. This is the highest they have been in over a decade. These Russian sales have helped compensate for lower free world production. Now consider column four. This column shows the shortfall of gold as made up by official sales. Note that since 1973, official sales have grown each year to a high in 1978 of 362 million ounces. This means, in effect, that in 1978 the demand for gold was 362 metric tons greater than the total world supplies of new gold. If there had not been official sales, the price surely would have been driven up enormously. As of this writing it appears that the shortfall in 1979 will be considerably higher even than that of 1978.

There are many ways to look at statistics. It's been often said, in fact, that you can prove anything you want by using the same set of figures. Nevertheless, this particular set of figures indicates to my thinking that, first, there is a shortage of *new* gold on the market and, second, the market itself is very thin. It can easily be influenced by relatively small purchases or sales. All of which is to say the price can shoot up (or down) *far and fast* as influenced by factors such as those discussed here. A shrewd investor will pay close attention to the supply/demand balance of gold.

4

Gold—past
and future price

We've had a chance to see where gold comes from and what influences its price today. Those are very valuable factors in our determination of whether gold is likely to go up or down in price tomorrow. However, there is another perspective that is equally valuable. That is to take a glance at what the price of gold has done in the past. How did gold get to be where it is today and what does that history tell us it is likely to do tomorrow?

For our purposes, we need not go further back than the turn of the century. The year was 1900. In that year the Gold Standard Act was passed. It had an enormous influence on the later price of gold. The Act, basically, said that each U.S. dollar must be backed by 24⅘ grains of 90 percent pure gold. The Act put the U.S. firmly on the gold standard.

It may come as a shock to some to learn that the U.S. was not on the gold standard until this century. It's really not surprising, however. Although the U.S. was a bit late in going on the gold standard, most of the world wasn't on it until the middle of the last century. Backing currency by gold was a relatively modern phenomenon. And, given our current problems with inflation it may seem like it was a very prudent thing to do. However, it wasn't so much wisdom that caused the early legislators to enact a gold standard act as necessity.

You'll recall in earlier chapters we were speaking of the great gold rushes of the 1800s. For a moment, let's consider two of them, the one in the western United States and the other in Australia.

While the gold from the western United States flowed mainly into the U.S. Treasury to be stored at various sites including the basement of the Denver Mint (where much of it still resides today), gold from Australia flowed into England and other European countries. Soon these countries as well as the United States were bulging with gold. The British, who at the time still had a viable world empire, were constantly seeking ways to strengthen their interests. One way was to make the pound a readily accepted currency anywhere in the world (much in the same fashion that the U.S. dollar is accepted today). To strengthen the pound, the British hit upon the idea of tying it to gold. It required no sacrifice on the part of England since the Treasury was already filled with the precious metal from Australia.

Once England went on the gold standard, the other European countries, in order not to have their own currencies fall in desirability relative to the British, soon joined the gold bandwagon. Germany went on gold next, then France, and soon most of the remaining European countries. Currency backed by gold was what each country insisted on in foreign trade. (Backed by gold essentially meant that the government would redeem any currency upon the bearer's demand in gold bullion at a fixed rate.)

This left the U.S. at a disadvantage. The U.S. had both gold and silver circulating coins (not to mention copper), but its currency was not backed by gold. (Rather it was backed by a combination of the good credit of the U.S. government and silver.)

Sentiment for putting the U.S. on the gold standard grew in

the late 1800s in order to make the U.S. a strong foreign trade competitor. However, there was also strong opposition. This was led primarily by the great U.S. silver interests and included owners of the many U.S. silver mines including those of the Comstock. They wanted the U.S. to remain on silver and, in fact, in 1890 had pushed through Congress the Sherman Silver Purchase Act which guaranteed that the U.S. government would buy not less than 4½ million ounces of new silver per year.

The two conflicting interests reached a climax in the presidential campaign of 1896. William Jennings Bryan, backed by the silver interests, made precious metal his main campaign issue. His fiery "Cross of Gold Speech" in which he said, ". . . you shall not crucify mankind on a cross of gold," was acclaimed as one of the finest American speeches ever delivered and is still studied today by students of history as well as those in the field of speech.

Yet, for all his oratory, Bryon lost and four years later the Gold Standard Act was legislated by Congress.

For years after this act the price of gold fixed by the U.S. government was low, reaching $20.67 an ounce into the 1920s. This worked a hardship on U.S. gold mining interests which found that as they moved into this century, they could not produce for that price. The cost of production moved beyond the price the U.S. was willing to pay. The mining industry pleaded for a gold subsidy as had been given in Australia. But, the pleas fell on deaf ears.

During this time most people forget or simply are unaware that the U.S. government was still regularly minting gold coins. These included the double eagle ($20 gold piece), the eagle ($10), the half eagle ($5), the quarter eagle ($2.50), and even a 1 dollar piece.

These were not small issue collector coins. They were regularly circulating gold coins issued in enormous quantities. Here are the mint figures for $20 gold coins during the 1920s.

After the 1929 stock market crash and the Great Depression, gold took on a new importance. The average U.S. citizen entered an era not only of great economic distress, but also of great

CHART 4A   U.S. $20 (DOUBLE EAGLE) GOLD COIN
(Mintage figures during the 1920s)

1920	228,350
1920S	558,000
1921	528,500
1922	1,375,500
1922S	2,658,500
1923	566,000
1923D	1,702,250
1924	4,323,500
1924D	3,049,000
1924S	2,917,500
1925	2,831,750
1925D	2,938,500
1925S	3,776,500
1926	816,750
1926D	481,000
1926S	2,041,500
1927	2,946,750
1927D	180,000
1927S	3,107,500
1928	8,816,000
1929	1,779,750
1930S	74,000
1931	2,938,250
1931D	106,500
1932	1,101,750
Total	51,843,600

Note: This coin was first minted in 1849 and last minted in 1933.
The "D" or "S" after the date indicates the mint where the coin was struck. "D" indicates the Denver Mint, "S" the San Francisco Assay Office, and no letter indicates the coin was struck at the Philadelphia Mint.

financial fear. With businesses and banks going broke everywhere, with millions unemployed and more being laid off daily, the average person sought economic refuge. One course that was taken was to hoard money. Money was taken out of banks, which as they collapsed made the average person fear them even more and as money was withdrawn made them more likely to collapse. The money was frequently stored against the future which most feared would be even bleaker. The most convenient way of storing that money was in the form of coinage. The most valuable coinage was gold. In mattresses, in tin cans buried in the ground, in chests hidden behind the stove, everyone held what gold they could afford. It seemed the safest, most prudent thing to do.

But, what may have been wise for the individual, was a disaster for the country as a whole. Economic health depended on a good circulation of money. Withdrawing money from circulation had the effect of cutting down on consumption. Reduced consumption (retail purchases of products) reduced the number of products bought at wholesale and eventually the number manufactured. This resulted in layoffs which, in great numbers, lowered the overall ability of consumers to make more purchases. The effect was to, if not create, at least deepen the depression. (This is the opposite of what the country faced in the period 1975 through 1979.)

One method of getting the economy going again was to place more money in circulation. President Franklin D. Roosevelt acted to do this in 1933. He outlawed gold ownership by private citizens. Any gold (other than rare coins, those with numismatic value) was confiscated by the Federal government.

The effects of this action were two-fold. First, they cut down on hoarding. Second, they gave the government new gold upon which it could issue more paper money. This ability to issue paper money was substantially increased when the government reduced the gold content of its paper. In conjunction with this the price of gold was raised to 35 U.S. dollars to 1 ounce.

Some readers may be expressing surprise at my tone in the last few paragraphs. I seem to be championing the cause of increased paper dollars at a time when we all know that increased paper dollars have led to their reduction in value—to inflation which has come to be the great evil of the last decade.

The important thing to remember here, however, is that we're talking from the perspective of the depression. We're talking of a period when rather then buying less, the dollar actually was buying *more!* The problem during the Great Depression was not too many dollars, as it is today, but too few. The solution, therefore, was the opposite of the solution to our present financial crisis. In the depression the need was to get more dollars into circulation rather than less. (It was not until the Second World War when the U.S. went into enormous deficit spending that this was accomplished and, as a result, the economy finally boomed.)

Starting with 1933, U.S. citizens, therefore, were not allowed to own bullion gold. All those gold coins which the U.S. mint had turned out prior to then were sent back to the Treasury where they were melted down into 300-ounce bars of roughly .900 fineness or 90 percent pure. (You'll recall that we said good delivery bars in London are usually .959 fineness or higher. This means that the majority of U.S. gold holdings do not meet world standards. When the U.S. auctions off its gold, therefore, frequently it commands a price slightly less than the going price for world gold.) These gold bars were then stored in vaults primarily at Fort Knox and at the Federal Reserve in New York and form the basis of the U.S. gold reserve.

The Second World War, as we noted, tore the U.S. out of the Great Depression, but it also had an enormous effect on the role of gold for this country into the remainder of this century.

While World War II caused an economic boom here, it caused economic catastrophe abroad. The war was fought on the soil of Europe. After the war there was not a single European country whose ability to act as an industrial nation was not destroyed or severely impaired. The countries of Europe could not sustain themselves economically. They had to buy food, clothing, materials to build housing and to rebuild their industries. But this posed a financial problem. With what would they pay for their needs?

Their first purchases were made with francs, deutsche marks, pounds, and all the European currencies. But, what could the U.S. in turn buy from Europe? While European countries wanted dollars to purchase U.S. products, Americans had little use for European currencies. The result was that the value of the European currencies was severely threatened.

It's hard to remember now, but at one time, the U.S. dollar

was king abroad. A dollar in Europe could have bought a fine meal or even a night's lodging. Today, it can cost $10 just to buy a soft drink in parts of France.

The problems of a dollar-short Europe had been foreseen by government economists before the end of the war. In 1944 in Bretton Woods, New Hampshire, a conference was held to plan finances for a post-war world. Amongst other things to come out of the conference was the International Monetary Fund (IMF) and the agreement to use the U.S. dollar as the reserve currency of the world. What this meant, essentially, was that the U.S. government would guarantee the stability of the dollar and all the European currencies could then float in relation to it. In other words, the U.S. wouldn't use the advantage it had economically to destroy Europe financially.

To guarantee the stability of the dollar, the U.S. government agreed to exchange dollars for gold supplied by European governments at a fixed rate of $35 to 1 troy ounce and not to vary that exchange rate. It has been argued that this agreement alone saved Europe. European countries could obtain dollars for their gold reserves at a fixed rate. That meant that even though their demand for dollars was great, the price for obtaining them wouldn't change. The U.S. government was refusing to let the law of supply and demand operate. It was refusing to let the price of dollars increase.

In addition, in a display of unprecedented generosity, through the Marshall plan and other foreign aid programs, the U.S. freely pumped dollars overseas. The result was the rapid rebuilding of western Europe. Within five years after the war, Europe was virtually self-sufficient. Within ten years it was ready to challenge the U.S. economy.

The rebuilding process, however, had been costly for Europe. It had cost gold which was now in U.S. vaults. It is estimated that by the mid-1950s the United States had three-fourths of the free world's gold stored in reserves.

Fortunately, before Europe went gold-broke, it recovered. Soon, spurred on by sales of cameras, autos, and a thousand other items, the U.S. was buying as much from Europe as

Europe was buying from us. For a short time, the gold supply in both continents stabilized. This was in the mid-1950s.

Any reasonable government, at this period, would have patted itself on the back for a job well done and discontinued the freeze on the price of gold. However, in a display of economic disinterest that was later to prove very costly, the U.S. continued its fixed-rate gold policy.

Soon foreign economies began surging ahead of the United States. Since they had all rebuilt within the previous 10 years, they tended to be using newer, more efficient equipment than their American counterparts. The Europeans became more productive and soon we found it was cheaper to buy European (and Japanese) than American. Now the tables were turned. Instead of Germany wanting more dollars, the U.S. wanted more deutsche marks. The same was true of the other countries. Now the U.S. was in a position of wanting foreign currency. But, the U.S. economy was not devastated as had been Europe's. We could easily have brought the supply and demand of currency back into balance by lowering the value of the dollar in relation to foreign currencies. This would have made foreign currencies more valuable and thereby foreign products more expensive. Fewer would have been imported and a kind of equilibrium reached. The intensity of growth of Europe would have slowed, but then it was already largely recovered. But, the U.S. staunchly refused to consider dollar devaluation.

At home, in the meantime, another economic problem was occurring, inflation. The government knew from the Great Depression that increasing the money supply would pull the country out of an economic downturn. Therefore, every time there was a downturn, regardless of how slight, more money was created. What the government did not then realize (but which we today all too well know) is that creating more money artificially increases consumer spending. The demand for goods and services increases. Without any corresponding increase in supply, prices go up. Increasing the money supply causes inflation.

In addition, the late 1950s and early 1960s was an era of social concern in the country. Massive spending programs were inaugurated to help the disadvantaged. The cry was, "We can afford it." Whether or not the programs did any good aside, we certainly couldn't afford it. The massive programs were financed largely through deficit spending at the federal level—that meant more dollars created . . . and more inflation.

Soon foreign governments didn't want our currency at the price we said it was worth. They had high productivity and low inflation. We had relatively lower productivity and higher inflation. We could have simply devalued the dollar. But, that would have meant those cheap foreign products wouldn't be so cheap anymore. Instead, the U.S. began paying out gold to foreign governments. At the fixed rate of 35 U.S. dollars to an ounce, European governments which once turned in gold, now turned in dollars and received their gold back. Instead of becoming alarmed that the system intended to save Europe economically was now artificially propping up the dollar, nearly all Americans remained unconcerned and bought foreign products cheaply. Most felt that it was just a temporary imbalance anyway. We had received European gold, now we were giving it back. What harm could there be in that?

The harm, of course, was that we were artificially propping up the dollar.

In 1954 an event occurred which was to have a later profound effect on the dollar fiction the U.S. was creating. In 1954 the London free gold market was once again allowed to open. Of course, with the U.S. setting the official rate for gold, the price on the London market did not move much, at first. It was simply a convenience so that private individuals and private banks as well as governments could buy and sell gold.

However, as the U.S. appetite for cheap foreign goods (they weren't really cheap—we were buying them with gold) and relatively higher inflation continued, a strange thing happened.

One day in October of 1960 the London free gold market's price for the precious metal hit $40 a troy ounce, even though the U.S. was willing to sell at $35. The private demand was stronger than the government supply.

Rather than take the event as an alarm ringing, the U.S. government assumed it was an aberration in the private market. A temporary shortage. To avoid panic caused by any future price surge, under pressure from the U.S., the eight major gold-holding countries of the world agreed to a "pooling" of gold resources whereby they would take gold from their reserves and sell it in the private market if the price ever got higher than the established $35 an ounce and buy it if its value ever declined below that figure.

The new system worked well to stabilize the price of gold, for a while. At first the pool was able to buy when supply was high and sell when supply was low. After 1966, however, the value of dollars overseas had become so low and their numbers so great, that the price could not be easily supported in the private gold market. The pool was only supplying gold to maintain the $35 price, never having an opportunity to buy because the price never got lower.

In the meantime, the U.S. gold stockpile continued to decline. Then, in 1967, a real crisis occurred. The British devalued the pound sterling by almost 15 percent and in reaction, investors and bankers fled the sterling into gold.

The price for gold on the private market soared. (Remember, in Europe private individuals were not prohibited from owning gold as they were in the U.S.) In order to keep the price of gold from rising above $35 an ounce, the U.S. and the other major gold-holders had to pour an estimated 3 billion dollars worth of gold into the private market over a 5 month period. It was now evident to even the most casual observer that the system could not endure.

In mid-1968 representatives of the major gold-holding nations met in Washington, D.C., and created a "two-tier" system.

Under this system, governments would continue to exchange gold between each other in payment for currency imbalances. This was one tier. On the other tier, the private price of gold could rise and fall at will without interference. Whereas before, the countries agreed to sell and buy gold to stabilize the market, they now agreed not to buy or sell no matter what the private market did.

It is crucial to understand that within a year of this agreement, South Africa reached agreement with the gold-holding countries to allow it to sell either directly to governments or on the open market—at its option.

Armageddon for the U.S. gold supply was rapidly drawing close. Even with the two-tier system, the U.S. was rapidly losing its gold supply. By 1971 we were down to about ⅓ of the supplies during the years of our highest reserves.

One might think that this amount of gold left was substantial enough to last for many years. But, that is without taking into account the Gold Reserve Act. Nearly all of the gold left in the U.S. vaults was already pledged as a backing for much of our currency!

As a result of the U.S. government's refusal to let the dollar depreciate in value, then-President Nixon on August 15, 1971, was forced to take the U.S. off the gold standard. Within a few months a meeting was called to reconcile the monetary differences between countries. Called the Smithsonian meeting, it resulted in a forced devaluation of the dollar to an official rate of $38 to 1 ounce of gold (later further devalued to $42). At the meeting, members of the International Monetary Fund (which had been created in 1944 in Bretton Woods) agreed to honor that official rate in essence even without a free exchange of gold. Also created at the meeting were plans for Special Drawing Rights (SDR). This quickly became dubbed "paper gold." SDRs originally represented gold sent to the IMF by each member nation—it was a sort of gold backed international currency. Later, however, they became an average of sixteen of the world's strongest currencies. (Russia was not included because, as we noted in the last chapter, it was not a member of the IMF.) The sixteen currencies were weighted and averaged and then each country, depending on its contribution, received so many SDRs. It could then use these to rectify any currency imbalances. It was a new approach to international finance.

At about the same time, because the U.S. went off the gold standard imposed back in 1900, the remaining massive U.S. gold stockpile was freed. It no longer was tied to the dollar.

All these events, dramatic though they may have been, did not settle the gold market down. By the end of 1971 the free market price of the precious metal was about $44 an ounce. By the end of 1972 it had risen to over $65 an ounce.

For a time, the IMF plan did seem to work. There was no international financial collapse. Countries did accept each other's currencies. In fact, the world was relatively stable. About this time, the U.S. broke its final ties with gold. The dollar was allowed to float against other currencies and not be tied to a fixed rate of gold.

In the spirit of this stability, the U.S. decided to prove once and for all that its new non-gold monetary policy would succeed. By congressional vote and presidential signature, the U.S. citizen for the first time in over forty years was to be given the right to own and hold bullion gold. The date for the historic event was January 1, 1975.

I can recall the days before New Years, 1975, vividly. Gold, which by the beginning of 1974 was well above $100 an ounce, began to creep upward in price in anticipation of the expected big new American market. It was widely felt that once Americans were allowed to own gold, they would make massive purchases sending the price soaring upward by their demand. Gold bugs, or those who believed in the precious metal, were predicting the price would top $500 an ounce by the end of 1975. It was indeed an exciting time.

I myself was involved in editing a magazine optimistically entitled, *Goldrush of 1975*. We were printing hundreds of thousands of copies to distribute to newsstands across America. The issue would inform the public about the gold legalization act as well as offer hints on what types of gold to buy.

I and the rest of the staff watched the price of gold edge upward throughout the last half of 1974. Enterprising individuals began opening gold dealerships throughout the country to be able to handle gold sales on the very first day of legalization. Those who experienced it said it was a feeling similar to when prohibition was repealed. And the price of gold responded. A few days before the end of the year it topped $200 an ounce on several markets. It was an historic occasion and an auspicious way to enter the new golden age for America.

Nineteen seventy-five dawned bright and clear. We all awaited the anticipated new gold rush. It never came. People went about their business just as they had done in 1974. True, there were some stories on TV and in the paper about gold, but hardly anyone paid attention. After all, no one in America had bought gold in 40 years. That was something Europeans did.

Due to lack of interest the much-anticipated American market failed to materialize. Dealers closed their doors. Banks, which had been prepared to sell gold ingots, sent back their supplies. And our magazine sat on the newsstands with few buyers.

The price of gold took the news hard. It began to fall, a long, downward plunge. The disinterest of the Americans seemed to discourage European investors and hoarders. They began to wonder that perhaps the new non-gold monetary system really would work. As if to give added concern to their worries, the U.S. government announced two major gold auctions, open to anyone who could buy 400-ounce bars.

Here was the American government brazenly willing to sell its once-cherished gold reserve on the open market. It was not the size of the sales which impressed the world. It was the fact that the U.S. was willing to sell at all.

The price decline for gold continued until about August of 1976 when it reached a low of nearly $106 an ounce. This was a critical point for gold. Although it is difficult to find official confirmation, apparently during the recession in 1974 and 1975, the Italian government obtained enormous loans from Germany. As a guarantee for that money, the Italian government apparently pledged its gold holdings valued at a minimum of $125 U.S. an ounce. When the price of gold fell below that, the entire loan structure was threatened.

Governments rarely announce what they are going to do in international finance. They almost as rarely tell what they have done. It is believed by several experts that in order to steady the price of gold in 1976, the German government surrepticiously bought gold on the open market.

In any event, from a low of $106 in 1976, gold began a slow, but steady increase in price that lasted through early 1979. That price increase is shown in Chart 4B.

CHART 4B THE PRICE OF GOLD (derived from an average of monthly prices based on London gold fixings supplied by Mocatta Metals Corp.)

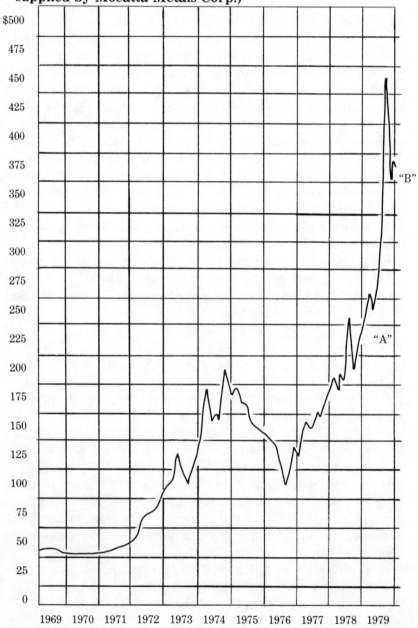

Note that the price is not a steady line upward, but a series of ragged edges, some up, some down. This, as we noted in the last chapter, is the way the price of gold moves in response to supply and demand as it seeks equilibrium. The important thing to notice is the overall direction of the price, not any particular moment in time.

While the price has gone up, there are two areas that we need to pay special attention to. They are market "A" for the end of 1978 and "B" for the end of 1979.

"A"

In November, 1978, there was a steep drop in the price of gold. Although that drop was almost immediately reversed, it is significant and has great import for what could happen to gold again in the future. Before explaining that drop, however, we need to say a few words about the steady increase in the gold price from 1976 through 1978.

The Vietnam War had a major effect on the U.S. dollar. Because it was largely an unpopular war, it was fought without big tax increases to pay for it. The U.S. government paid for the war by increasing the federal debt—it was a war paid for by borrowing. The result was many more dollars of much less value—inflation.

In addition, the Arab oil cartel in 1974 imposed stringent price increases on oil. This added to inflation. It had another serious effect, however. In order to buy oil, we had to send dollars abroad. Led by oil imports our trade figures went way out of balance. We were importing much more than we were exporting. (Americans had not lost their appetite for foreign goods. They were purchasing them in far larger numbers than foreigners were purchasing American goods.)

The overall result was that suddenly there was an enormous glut of dollars abroad. The term "Euro-dollar" became fashionable. It simply meant U.S. dollars located in Europe. By the end of 1978 there were estimated to be an incredible $600 billion Euro-dollars.

As the supply of dollars increased, their value relative to

foreign currency decreased. People had little use for dollars. They wanted deutsche marks, Swiss francs—and gold.

The value of all these currencies moved up relative to the dollar. Because some Europeans were turning to gold as a further dollar alternative, the price of gold also climbed steadily.

Thinking back to September and October of 1978, I can recall the atmosphere of crisis in the air. The opening news story on television each night was the falling U.S. dollar. Europeans by the millions were quickly cashing in their dollars before they fell even further and this, of course, caused the price to decline ever more swiftly. Banks were accused of profiting from the currency market by dumping huge quantities of dollars and later buying back at lower prices. Something had to be done or, it was feared, the free world would be thrown into financial chaos.

At the end of October 23, 1978, then President Jimmy Carter acted. He inaugurated a $30 billion program to buy back U.S. dollars. In addition, he announced new monthly sales of U.S. gold to begin immediately in the amounts of 1.5 million ounces per month.

The apex of the gold price chart (Chart 4B) in the area circled by "A" is the very day of President Carter's announcement. The dollar strengthened relative to foreign currencies while gold plunged precipitously. The announcement that the U.S. would significantly increase the gold supply coupled with the strengthening of the dollar wounded gold.

At the time, many thought the wound would be fatal. The basic problems with the dollar, however, had not been healed— only bandaged. When this became apparent even before 1978 ended, gold began a strong surge upward again. In the hindsight it turned out that gold had only been bruised by the U.S. moves.

"B"

Now, let's consider the area of the chart marked "B." This was the period roughly 1 year later when gold skyrocketed to an incredible $444 an ounce before plunging back down through the $400 barrier. The circumstances were a bit different this time.

As noted, the sick dollar was gradually forcing the price of gold up. In early 1979, however, the OPEC nations announced a new and very steep increase in the price of oil. (It was argued that this price increase was precipitated by U.S. inflation.)

This new price increase had a dramatic, but different, effect on world currencies and gold. To understand it one must recall that one of the world's largest oil producers is the United States. On the other hand, Europe and Japan, the other leading industrialized areas of the world, have virtually no oil production (with the exception of Britain's North Sea oil). A steep price increase in oil prices left the U.S., because of its domestic oil, in a *relatively* better position than the rest of the industrialized nations of the world.

In a wave of fear, Europeans and other currency investors began buying dollars. The currency markets in the months of March, April, and May of 1979 were as easy to understand as oil. Countries with oil had strong currency. Countries without had weak currency. This carried over into gold. With the dollar strengthening, people began switching to it from gold. As more gold came onto the market, the price edged lower. This can be seen on Chart 4B as the dip early in 1979.

European countries, particularly Germany, however, immediately anticipated what increased oil prices meant. It meant increased inflation. Germany immediately raised interest rates as a method of cutting back on the money supply to reduce inflation. Other European countries followed suit. The U.S., however, did little, immediately.

During the summer of 1979, American business people, quite well aware by this time of the economic consequences of oil price boosts, saw what was happening. They realized that inflation was bound to hit the U.S. and hard. And they knew from past experience that one tried and true method of dealing with it was to increase interest rates. Since much higher interest rates could not be far off, these business people pushed forward borrowing which they planned to make. Instead of waiting until later in the year to borrow or increase inventories and capital expansion, they borrowed immediately.

Through a complicated process, our fractional reserve banking system actually creates new money through such borrowing. (For a detailed explanation of this process I suggest, *Buying and Selling Currency for Profit*, Contemporary Books, 1979.) In other words, new credit can cause increased money supply. Suddenly through May, June, July, and August, the money supply in the U.S. increased enormously. This, as we've noted, acts to trigger more inflation which, when coupled with the oil price increase pushed the inflation figures to 12 and 13 percent. The U.S., because the government had not acted promptly to raise interest rates immediately after the oil price boost and to control the money supply, was staggering under the worst inflation since the Second World War.

For just a moment now, let's change perspective. Let's consider the way the oil-producing nations view the U.S. They have just instituted a significant oil price increase. They are getting more dollars back for their oil. But, suddenly, the U.S. goes into hyper-inflation. Those dollars that they are receiving back are worth much less. The oil producers have been partially frustrated in their attempts to get more *real* wealth for their oil. What can they do?

For one thing, they can raise the price of oil even higher. But, this is likely to produce even more dollar inflation meaning they'll get paid in even less valuable dollars. Not a good alternative.

Another alternative (there are several others including refusing to accept dollars for oil, but instead insisting on a basket of different currencies) is to buy gold. Gold has been going up in *real* value. It has been estimated that in 1975 1 troy ounce of gold would buy about 10 barrels of oil. By 1979 1 troy ounce would buy over 15 barrels of oil.

If the dollars received for oil were quickly converted to gold, then the oil producers would be receiving real wealth for their product. Apparently in September of 1979, this is exactly what several individuals decided to do. They bought gold.

But, they did not buy much gold. Perhaps not more than 5 or 10 percent of their dollar income in gold. (Remember, total dollar income from oil is in the hundreds of billions of dollars.)

As we noted in earlier chapters, the gold market is very thin. Gold supplies from both new and old sources can barely meet current demand. Add to the demand by petro-dollars converted to gold and the price can go through the roof. It did.

During the middle of 1979 gold was already going up because of the U.S. inflation. As soon as oil interests apparently entered the market, the price took off. From the middle of August through the end of September, the price rose nearly $100 an ounce! That was nearly a one-third increase in just a few months. Gold seemed destined to hit at least $500 an ounce by year's end.

It was at this time that the butcher, the baker, and the candlestick maker particularly in Europe began digging out the gold bars and coins from safety deposit vaults and selling. Gold had gone crazy and they were determined to take advantage of what seemed ridiculously high prices. More and more gold came onto the market as the price got higher (a phenomenon we noted in the last chapter on economics).

It was a wild market, a bubble that had to burst. It did in the first weeks of October. Over-heavy from the sheer weight of the gold brought onto the market and triggered by news of Russian wheat purchases, the price collapsed. It dropped $60 dollars in six days. That is the plunge noted on our chart by "B."

However, the fundamental reasons for gold's price increase remained—high U.S. inflation and petro-dollars. As this became apparent, gold stabilized.

The future

Having come this far, what is gold going to do now?

As of this writing the Federal Reserve has taken significant actions to reduce the expansion of the money supply and reduce inflation. The discount rate has been raised to historic levels and some reserve requirements have been raised. These are strong medicines and if allowed to do their work could have a beneficial effect on the U.S. economy.

On the other hand, cutting down on the money supply ultimately results in increased unemployment and recession. Strong medicine is hard to take when an unsympathetic electorate wants jobs.

In addition, OPEC has shown little patience with America's economic problems. Instead, it has repeatedly increased oil prices in an almost irresponsible manner. Each time it does so, it pushes inflation up another notch regardless of what the Federal Reserve does.

Putting it all together, what will the price of gold do in the future?

At this point, the reader should carefully note that the following constitutes nothing more than an educated guess. It should not be considered a recommendation of any kind. The reader should not make any investment without first consulting with his or her attorney or other professional financial advisor.

If OPEC continues its past tradition of price increases, and barring any unlikely *sudden, steep* decline in the U.S. inflation rate or any new, very large gold sales, I believe the price of gold will eventually continue to rise. The rise will not be steady, but will have many peaks and dips as we've seen in the past, but the overall trend should be upward in the future.

Barring those events just noted, my own opinion is that by the end of 1980 gold will be maintaining at least a $400 price level. By the end of 1981 I believe it could be maintaining a $500 level and by 1985 it could be as high as $750 an ounce. (In the meantime, however, it could dip as low as $300 an ounce.)

I must, however, further qualify the above educated guesses. Going back to Chart 4B, it should be noted that *any* of those factors which influence gold prices down, such as Russian gold sales, could lower the price. Similarly, any of those factors which influence the price to go up, such as new investor interest or a war in South Africa interrupting gold supplies, could cause the price to rise.

Ultimately, no one knows what gold will do in the future. In the past the vast majority of experts, including myself on one or two occasions, have been wrong—and I'm the first to point this out. We are living in a volatile age and gold is a volatile commodity. Therefore my best suggestion to you the reader is to obtain your own information on what is happening in gold and draw your own conclusions. In other words, become your own expert.

Intervention

We've already seen that the U.S. government on occasion will sell gold on the open market from its vast stockpile. The usual reason for the sales is to increase the supply of gold, thereby reducing the price. This effort to influence gold's price on the free market could be correctly termed, intervention. The U.S. government is intervening for its own interests.

The U.S. government sales, though significant, are perhaps a mild form of intervention compared with what the government could and might do sometime in the future. I am referring to the confiscation of all bullion gold owned by citizens.

It might not be worth mentioning except for the fact that the U.S. government already has acted to confiscate gold, as we saw, back in 1933. If government leaders feel the economy of the country is threatened and think that eliminating private owner-ship of gold would help that economy, they have precedent on their side in ordering a gold prohibition.

In any general delegalization of gold, there are probably two alternatives the government could use in its program. One would be to simply buy the gold from U.S. citizens at a fixed rate per ounce. The other would be a general confiscation in which the government might issue certificates indicating how much gold was turned in and which would entitle the owner to the return of the gold at a future date.

Either alternative must be of concern to the gold investor. In the first case, if the price set by the government were lower than the price paid for the metal by the investor, he or she would lose the difference outright. In the latter case with confiscation and certificates, the cost of the gold would be tied up indefinitely while the price might plummet. And, of course, there is the consideration that the government might never return the gold.

This problem of intervention is not mentioned to scare potential investors, but to alert them to what may be a remote, but a real possibility. When investing in gold, unforseen intervention, just as theft, offers the possibility of wiping out both potential profits and capital. It is a risk that most investors are willing to take. But, after 1933, it simply can't be ignored.

Sources of information

For additional or more current information, check these items. (Note: Some are free, others can be fairly expensive—write the publishers for current prices.)

CM REPORT
Chamber of Mines of South Africa
5 Holland St.
Johannesburg, S.A.

FEDERAL RESERVE BULLETIN AND CHART BOOK
   ($20 for bulletin, $7 for chart books annually)
Board of Governors of the Federal Reserve
Washington, DC 20551
(These publications contain information and graphs on economic conditions in the U.S.)

THE GOLD NEWS
Suite 1140
1001 Connecticut Ave.
Washington, DC 20036
(Contains information on new uses of gold as well as occasional statistics on gold supply and demand.)

INTERNATIONAL MONETARY FUND
INTERNATIONAL FINANCIAL STATISTICS (about $35
  annually)
Secretary, IMF
Washington, DC 29431
(Gives international economic statistics.)

THE WALL STREET JOURNAL (about $50 annually)
22 Cordlandt St.
New York, NY 10007
(Published daily except Saturday and Sunday, it is a financial education in itself.)

5

Making a profit on gold

The way to make a profit on gold is to buy low and sell high. (We'll consider the futures market, where this rule does not always apply, in Chapter 6.)

What could be simpler? As we noted earlier, there is a lot of treacherous territory between buying and selling for profit. There's the matter of the proper investment strategy. Consider a friend of mine, Harry.

Harry had heard that gold was going wild in price. Every other day he read that it was reaching new historic highs. He knew of people who were making fortunes in the market. "If they can, why can't I?" he asked himself.

Harry decided to join the gold bandwagon. He bought.

Unfortunately, soon after Harry bought, the price of gold leveled off, then started down. (As we've seen, while gold's trend may be upward, its progress is a series of ups and downs or see-saw movements.) Each day Harry watched as the price deteriorated. He counted off the money he was losing and despaired.

"Why didn't I put my money in a nice safe savings account?" he asked himself. True, the interest paid to him would have been low, but his money would still be there. "Why did I get into gold?" he asked himself.

As the price of gold continued down, Harry decided it was time to cut his losses and run. He sold.

Unfortunately, just about the time Harry sold, gold reached the floor of that particular market swing and the price started up again. Harry began tearing his hair as he watched the price rise and realized that each dollar up meant a dollar out of his pocket because he had sold. Finally, when gold reached a high above the point where he had first bought, he decided that the market had really turned around. Gold was truly taking off in value. He bought again. A few days later gold began a new plunge downward.

Harry was a bad investor. He listened to what his heart was telling him and not his mind. He knew there was profit to be made in gold, but he just couldn't quite make the right moves. Harry was the type of person who played "follow the leader." He was the sort who "joined the bandwagon." He wanted to be absolutely sure his investment was going to make money. So, he waited until money had been made by others *before* he invested.

Harry bought high and sold low. Many new gold investors do the same thing. They listen to and follow the crowd. But there is very little profit in buying high and selling low.

There is nothing new in the "buy low, sell high" investment philosophy. Nearly every investment counselor will advise it. What's tricky is acting upon this advice.

In order to buy low and sell high, you have to trust in yourself. You have to investigate a field, such as gold, and then determine *on your own* that the price is likely to go up. Then, and this is the critical decision for this chapter, you have to decide when the price is low and when it is high.

There are clues. The price is likely to be lowest when everyone else is selling. When the price of gold starts down, an investor who wants to enter the market and make a profit starts paying close attention. He watches it fall, gauging the size of each daily drop. When he judges that gold has just about bottomed out, he buys.

It takes courage to do this. Most of our investors' friends will probably be telling him that gold is no good anymore. They will say that it's obvious that gold isn't a good investment, after all, isn't the price falling?

It's at this point that our wise investor will be listening to his mind. It will be telling him that based on his own investigations and judgments, he believes gold is a good investment. It will be telling him not to listen to his friends. It will tell him to buy when everyone else is selling.

If he's correct, he will probably buy just before the bottom of a price valley. He will reap the benefits as the price begins to go up. He will watch dollars turn to profit.

Soon he will hear friends talking about what's happening in gold. He will see the media reporting the price increases and feel the excitement. He will know he's part of it because he already owns gold.

At some point, the very friend who told him to get out because the price was going down, may tell him he himself is getting in because the price is going up. Of course, this friend happens to be named Harry.

At this point, and because of what he has learned about gold, our smart investor will see that the price has run up as high as it's likely to go and will sell, perhaps before the market peaks. Harry may be laughing at him, for a while. But, our investor has sold high . . . and made a reasonable profit.

It's not easy to be this smart investor. It takes investigation, decision making, and guts. But, it is possible. The important thing is to remember not to invest in gold or anything else on the basis of rumor or "hot tips." Usually these are the worst kinds of investment advice. Become your own expert and then, trust your mind, not your heart.

Playing the gold field

There is another sort of problem that investors may face.

Occasionally a new investor will accidentally get into gold when it's low, wait until it goes up and then sell for a profit. While our investor is congratulating himself or herself, he or she may also be wondering if it's possible to do it again? In fact, is it possible to do it over and over again?

Repeated wins in the gold market are not only possible, they are, in fact, a method of increasing profit. However, with increased profits also go increased risks. Any investor who moves in and out of the market stands the risk of losing his shirt in a sudden turnaround or a bad guess. It's the dangerous way to buy bullion, but there could be bigger profit in it. Consider this hypothetical graph on gold's price:

CHART 5A *HYPOTHETICAL* GOLD PRICE INCREASE*

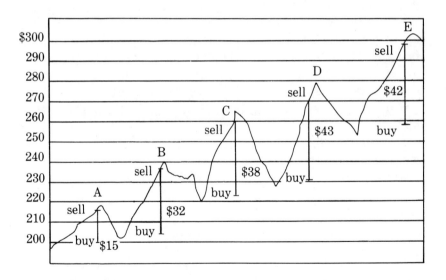

*Note: The prices on this chart are strictly theoretical. They do not reflect past, present, or future actual prices.

Our investor here, whom we'll call Clair, decided she wanted to make big profits in gold. She read books, learned about the market, talked with her attorney, and decided to buy. She bought when gold was about $200 and sold when it reached $215, before the peak (marked "A"). She bought again when gold dropped back to $206 (before the bottom) and sold again at about $238 (again, before the peak, "B"). She continued her gold purchases and sales marked "C," "D," and "E" each time missing the top and bottom of the market, but each time making a profit.

Because of her judicious investing, while gold went up $100 an ounce (from $200 to $300) Clair made nearly $170 per ounce on her investing—the profit of "A" plus "B" plus "C" plus "D" plus "E" ($15 + $32 + $38 + $43 + $42 = $170).

Clair was willing to risk losing big in order to win bigger.

Of course, it could be pointed out that there's no reason to lose at all, as long as gold eventually goes higher in price than what was paid for it. If you move in and out of the market and then guess wrong, you just stop playing until the price of gold catches up to you. The assumption, of course, is that this will take a fairly short time. Unfortunately, gold has, on occasion, plateaued for long periods, perhaps a year or more, without a significant price move upwards. (It could, in fact, continue downwards!)

Nonetheless, the whole point of bringing up the possibility of moving into and out of the market is to illustrate that buying gold need not be simply a single purchase and then years of waiting. It can be a series of purchases and sales. In a sense, the gold market can be played like the stock market.

Gold on borrowed money

This brings to mind another point. One should never invest in gold with borrowed money. Borrowed money requires repayment, usually within strict time limits. If the borrower guesses right and gold goes up, the loan can be quickly repaid and everything comes out well. On the other hand, if gold does not go up in price, the borrower may be stuck making payments on money stuck into a non-producing investment. Remember, gold, unlike real estate or stocks, for examples, does not show any return except upon sale. While you own it, it only costs you money (storage, insurance, etc.). It doesn't bring in any rents or dividends.

Costs of purchase

Back in Chapter 1 we discussed the premium that has to be paid when purchasing gold bullion coins, the most popular form of bullion investment. There are, however, other costs which should be considered. Though usually slight, there is the cost of storage. If this takes the form of a vault in a bank, it's the price of the vault.

Then there is insurance. Oftentimes it is difficult if not impossible to get insurance on a gold bullion investment. But, some investors do manage to search out insurance companies and find one or two who will insure them. The restrictions on the movement of gold are usually severe and the premium often very high.

Technical analysis

Thus far we've been looking mainly at those factors which "fundamentally" affect the price of gold. There's another whole realm of research called "technical analysis." This tends to look for patterns in gold's price.

Technical research is of particular importance to those investing in gold futures where a price variation of only a dollar or two can make a big difference in margin calls. It is a complex field and there have been whole books written on it alone. (Check with a good commodities broker for more information.)

Barriers

Technical analysis sometimes speaks of psychological price barriers. These are frequently round numbers such as $300 an ounce or $400 an ounce or $280 an ounce or any of a hundred others. For reasons that cannot be fully explained on fundamental grounds, the price sometimes has great difficulty in breaking through these barriers going either upward or downward. It may approach many times, only to withdraw. It is as if there is a wall through which the price cannot penetrate. This is sometimes called "resistance."

Of course, these barriers are all hypothetical. They do get broken, but when they do, it tends to lead to another phenomenon which might be termed "breakthrough." After succeeding in breaking the $300 barrier for the first time, for example, gold quickly penetrated upward toward $400. Its price seemed to run away until a new barrier was found.

Barriers are sometimes considered psychological in nature. They may, in fact, exist simply because buyers and sellers are afraid to buy and sell above or below them. They may be in effect, another manifestation of crowd psychology.

Patterns

Many people studying the price history of gold tend to see patterns. It's similar to our ancestors in an ancient world looking up at the heavens and seeing patterns in the stars. They saw archers and animals and other designs. The same seems to be true with gold's price. And just as many people today claim to have based successful actions on the stars, many gold investors claim profits based on patterns.

At one time, for example, people were pointing to the "orderly" price advance of gold. What they meant by this was that it appeared that each time gold dropped in price, it dropped only about half the previous rise, then it turned around and moved upward again. It was similar to saying that gold moved something like two steps forward, then one step back, with strict regularity.

For a time, in fact, particularly through 1977, this analysis did seem, in fact, to be accurate and some who bought and sold based on it actually may have made money. However, with the wild market of 1979, it pretty much went out the window.

The point is that while patterns obviously do exist, we don't know for how long they are going to exist. Acting on them alone, therefore, can become extremely risky.

There is a further study of price that tries to combine a technical analysis with fundamentals. When successful, this offers the most convincing sort of evidence for what gold is likely to do in the future. Consider this *hypothetical* example. Let's suppose that in examing the price of gold, we chance to notice that over the past three years, a sudden sharp price drop has occurred with regularity every five months followed by a slow return to previous price levels. (Starting with January, the next price drop was May, then October, then March, and so on.) The drop in each case was about $25. In trying to understand the reason for this drop we accidentally discover that at the beginning of each of those months, the Russians had sold large quantities of gold.

In this *hypothetical* example we've combined a pattern with fundamental knowledge. According to our pattern we believe that the Russians will sell gold every five months. We now consider acting on our knowledge during the next five-month period. (Of course, we don't really know that the Russians are selling this regularly. It may just be a coincidence. Or, even though they were selling regularly, they may decide not to sell this time. The Russians do not announce in advance when their gold sales will be.)

If we act on our belief, we will probably sell just before the anticipated drop and buy back later. If we are successful and do this every five months, we could very soon become wealthy indeed.

Have we solved the mystery of predicting the future price of gold? Not at all. The Soviets might suddenly decide not to sell every five months if they ever did. Or the pattern may be chance having nothing to do with Soviet sales. Or next month South Africa may suddenly reduce gold output causing the price to jump. It's still a risk. All that we've done by this double analysis is, hopefully, given ourselves an "edge" on the market.

How does an investor find those coincidences when fundamentals appear to line up with technical analysis? The investor studies the market.

The market changes constantly. What was true of it when these words were written, may no longer apply by the time you read them. An investor who seriously wants to get ahead of gold will talk with commodities brokers and gold dealers as well as study the price history of the precious metal. A good way to begin is to keep your own record of gold's price. Get some graph paper, draw the days of the month across the bottom, the price down the left side, and plot the changes in price on the graph. By doing this daily you'll become intimately familiar with what gold is currently doing. Eventually, you may discern some pattern which you may be able to line up with some fundamental. You'll have become your own expert. But remember, every expert knows that no matter how convincing the evidence may seem, it's still a risk.

6

Gold and the futures market

The futures market is a very exciting field. It is exciting, in part, because you don't have to pay the full price of the gold when a purchase is made. You can use leverage and pay only 5 percent or less of the price! Of course, there are additional risks.

The basic operation of the futures market is fairly simple. The investor contracts to either buy or sell gold at some future date. As proof of good intentions, the investor puts up a deposit. The deposit assures the other party to the contract (if you're the buyer, the other party is the seller and vice versa) that the investor will follow through. Eventually the investor sells or "closes out" the contract, hopefully, at a profit.

Perhaps the best way to get started in gold futures is to spend a little time (instead of money) investigating the field. Talk with several commodities brokers, write to the commodities exchanges for information (addresses are given at the end of this chapter) and read everything you can about the market. Commodity futures is a complicated subject and this short chapter will barely be able to skim the surface. It is so complex, in fact, that some people *never* comprehend it. If after reading, investigating, and talking to experts, you still don't understand what's happening, stay out! The commodities market offers investors unlimited potential for profit. For the unwary or unfortunate investor, however, it also offers UNLIMITED potential for loss!

I repeat, if after studying many sources, you still don't understand the market, stay out!

Having given that warning advice, let's probe the surface of gold commodities futures.

At the present time there are basically four commodities markets in the United States that handle gold futures. They are the International Monetary Market (IMM) of the Chicago Mercantile Exchange, the Commodity Exchange, Inc. (Comex), the Chicago Board of Trade, and the New York Mercantile Exchange.

It is important to know who handles gold contracts because each exchange may handle different size contracts and have different deposit requirements.

As a private individual, you cannot deal directly with the commodities exchange unless you purchase a seat on the floor of the exchange. This may cost $50,000 or more and hardly be worthwhile when starting out. Therefore you'll deal with a commodities broker. Finding a good broker is essential to having successful trades.

How do you know a good commodities broker? It's not always easy. He or she should have been in the business long enough to have made all the mistakes. That way the broker can save *you* from making them. I would think five years active commodity trading would be a minimum requirement. The broker should work for a firm large enough to have seats on various commodity exchanges so you can choose from a variety of contracts and so your orders can be placed without delay. It should be large enough to afford the latest computers which will show at a moment's glance the current and future prices of gold.

Besides experience and working for a substantial firm, your broker should be intelligent, aware of the market from moment to moment, and pleasant to talk with. These latter qualities you'll have to judge for yourself and a good way to do it is to go down to the broker's office on several occasions before buying anything and have chats with him or her. A good broker won't mind your taking up some time, provided you don't come early or late in the trading day when the market is likely to be most active.

While you're talking with your broker, listen carefully to what he or she says. Remember, a broker isn't paid a salary like a carpenter or a banker. He or she survives by making a commission on each transaction. Be a bit wary of brokers who try to get you into the market by suggesting that you quickly make a series of rapid-fire transactions. This may make you money, or, it might simply fatten the broker's commissions.

It's also important to remember that it is in the nature of commodities trading to deal with volatility. Prices move up and down not just on a daily basis, but on a moment-to-moment basis. And there are always tipsters around to fill your ears with the right answer to what's going to happen next. Be wary of such individuals, particularly if they wear broker's clothes. As we've noted earlier, no one knows what's going to happen in the future.

Unless you just want to have fun playing the futures market (and many people do) and can afford to hire a competent brokerage firm to manage an account for you, I suggest you spend a good deal of time personally investigating your prospective broker. Find someone you like and can trust and then work with him or her. You'll improve your chances considerably.

One last word of caution before we consider futures trading. This is a risky business. You can lose all your money by bad investment or you can see some of your profit and capital eaten away in broker's fees. This is not to say that you can't make big profits. You can. But, you can also make big losses. All of which goes to say that you shouldn't even think of entering the commodities market as a speculator (a term to be explained shortly) unless you enter it with high-risk money—money that you can afford to lose without affecting your style of life or your regular source of income. And never, never enter the market with borrowed money. (Generally speaking high-risk money is usually considered to be no more than 5 to 10 percent of your net worth.)

How much is a minimum investment? I've heard knowledgeable people say that one shouldn't enter the market with less than $50,000. Others emphasize that $5,000 is the minimum necessary. Usually the reason for giving minimums such as these is the fact that before you win, you may lose many times. And you will need sufficient capital to see you through the losses. As for myself, I don't feel that there is any minimum or maximum amount (other than the minimums set by brokerage firms), as long as you can afford to lose the money you invest, walk away, and not feel it's the end of the world. It's sort of the same psychology used in gambling. Never gamble with more than you can afford to lose.

If you haven't been discouraged by what's been said thus far, let's look at the market.

The commodities market

The commodities market is exactly what it says it is. A market to deal in commodities. Gold is a commodity just like plywood, orange juice, and pork bellies and is bought and sold on the market. However, unlike buying and selling the actual metal itself, on the commodities market an investor enters into a contract to either buy or sell gold *at some future date*. This is why it is called the futures market.

That future date could be next month or many months away. Perhaps the best way to explain the market is to take a highly simplified example. Let's say that an electronics assembling plant, which uses gold as part of its product, knows that it's going to need 100 ounces in two months. It doesn't need the gold today for its production, but, two months from today it will need it. Our assembler also knows that gold has been going up in price. If he waits two months to make a purchase, he may have to pay substantially more than if he bought today. On the other hand, if he buys today, he will be out the money the gold costs for the two month waiting period (100 ounces at $300 an ounce means an immediate investment of $30,000).

Our investor, of course, might be able to borrow $30,000 and buy the gold today paying interest on the borrowed money for two months, then repaying the loan with anticipated cash. But, borrowing offers certain risks also. What if the price of gold goes down in the next two months? Our assembler then is stuck with a $30,000 loan when, if he had waited, he might have been able to buy the gold two months from now for much less. There also would be the wasted interest charge for the extra money. Finally, what if our assembler can't swing a $30,000 commercial loan?

One answer is the futures market. Our investor enters into a contract whereby he agrees to buy gold, but not until two months from now. As part of the contract, he specifies the price he will pay. (The price of gold today is referred to as the "spot" price and is similar to the bullion price. The price two months from now is the "future" price and is usually somewhat higher based to a degree on the interest charges that it would have cost to have borrowed the money to have bought the gold for cash today.)

To show his good faith, our assembler puts up a deposit. On his intention to purchase $30,000 worth of gold, the deposit may be only $2,000 and may be refundable. We'll consider the deposit more in a moment. As a fee to the broker, our assembler probably pays under $100.

Now, let's consider a small private minting company that has been minting gold medallions. The company overbought gold and anticipates that in two months, it will have an oversupply of 100 ounces. The price today is $300 an ounce, but our minter is afraid that it may go down in the future. She would love to sell today, but is afraid that if she does so, it may turn out that in reality she will need the gold. She wants to play it safe. She wants to sell in two months, but she wants to sell at or close to today's spot price. Our minter enters into a contract to sell 100 ounces of gold two months in the future. She, like our assembler, also puts up a deposit of about $2,000.

What could be simpler? We have a gold buyer and a gold seller, one aggreeing to buy, the other to sell two months in the future. (By the way, these two participants are called "hedgers" in the market's parlance. They are hedging against real price rises or falls.) What complicates the simple procedure we've just described is price. Let's assume that the future price both parties agreed to was $310 an ounce for gold two months in the future. Now, let's further assume that one week after the contracts were entered into, the future price of gold jumped to $315 (because the spot price was up a similar amount). Note, that this is only an increase of $5 an ounce. What happens to our minter and our assembler?

Before we find out, it is important to understand that it is possible to "close out" a contract at almost any time (except when the market is up or down the limit, to be explained shortly). What this means is that a buyer can "offset" his buying contract by obtaining a selling contract. A seller can do the opposite. The contracts cancel each other out. Of course, they might be for different prices as the future price of gold changes and that leads us back to our assembler and our minter.

Our assembler is quite happy when gold goes up $5 an ounce. He has a contract which entitles him to buy gold at the set price of $310 an ounce. But, the future price of gold has gone to $315. He can, therefore, today obtain a contract to sell 100 ounces in the future at $315. The two contracts would offset one another, leaving our assembler with a profit of $5 per ounce ($315 an ounce less $310 an ounce equals a $5 profit). Since the contract was for 100 ounces he shows a quick, neat profit of $500.

However, our assembler doesn't even have to offset his contract to collect his $500. The money is added automatically to his original $2,000 deposit and he can withdraw it any time he wants!

Now, let's consider our minter. Things haven't gone quite so well for her. She agreed to sell at a future price of $310 an ounce. But, the future price has gone up to $315. If she sells at $310, she'll be losing $5 an ounce or $500. She might not want to sell at this kind of a loss. To insure her cooperation, the $500 loss she would incur by selling is immediately taken from that $2,000 deposit she originally put up. Where does it go? You're right, it goes to our assembler.

This, in its most simple form is how the futures market operates. The deposits put up guarantee that the buyer or the seller will follow through on the contract. That is how it is possible to buy or sell gold using only 5 percent or less of the actual price.

Deposit

Let's look a bit more closely at that deposit. It actually is comprised of two elements. One is the deposit itself. In our example, perhaps this amounted to $1,000. The other is a maintenance margin, perhaps another $1,000. When gold went up in price, $500 was taken out of our minter's maintenance margin and added to our assembler's maintenance margin.

But, let's say that instead of going up just $5 an ounce, gold went up $10 an ounce to $320. This would mean a loss for our seller of $1,000. It would wipe out the entire maintenance margin. At this point or even before, the broker would call the minter and tell her to quickly deposit another $1,000 in the account. It would be a "margin" call.

If our minter did this, the contract would remain open. If she did not or could not answer the margin call, the broker would immediately "close out" the contract. That is, he would obtain a buying contract for 100 ounces at $320 offsetting the selling contract at $310. Our minter would receive back the deposit of $1,000 but because of the price fluctuation would lose the maintenance margin amount of $1,000.

Let's consider that deposit she received back. The reason for this deposit (and, incidentally, both deposit and maintenance margin amounts are set by the commodities exchanges in cooperation with individual brokerage houses) is to give the broker a little leeway in obtaining an offsetting contract. Let's suppose that between the time the price went up to $320 and the time he calls our minter and finds out she won't answer the margin call, gold goes up another $10 to $330. If he can't sell until the price reaches $330, the loss is $20 an ounce. On 100 ounces, that's a $2,000 loss. It was covered, however, by the deposit and the maintenance margin. Our minter has lost every penny she put up and received nothing back. (On the other hand, our assembler shows a $2,000 profit.)

To help stabilize the market, there are "limits" imposed by each commodities exchange. This is the maximum price fluctuation gold can go up or down in one day. This allows brokers to contact buyers and sellers and to either meet margin calls or to get offsetting contracts.

Occasionally, however, gold will go the limit for each of many days. This happens when the price shoots up or shoots down. It means that a seller or a buyer might not be able to get out of the market via an offsetting contract until a much higher or lower stable price is reached. Let's say, for example, that suddenly gold shoots up to the $400 level. The market goes up the limit each day and our broker cannot offset our minter's contract until a price of $400 an ounce has been reached. Our minter has now lost $90 an ounce or on 100 ounces, a total of $9,000. But, her deposit was only $2,000? True, but she now owes the brokerage firm $7,000 more! (Our assembler has made $9,000 in profit and he wants his money.)

Such sudden price increases up or down the limit for several days are unusual, but they do happen, particularly when there is an international financial crisis as in October–November of 1978 and September–October of 1979.

That is why it is frequently said that the futures market offers unlimited potential for profit as well as for loss.

Thus far we've been speaking of hedgers, those who actually have a use for gold. There is another element to the market and that is the investor. In the commodities future market, the investor is called the "speculator."

Speculators

In our example, both our assembler and our minter did not want to bear the risk of a fluctuating price. They entered the market to avoid risk. Yet, the risk was still there. Who assumed the risk? The speculator.

Perhaps at this point several readers may be pointing out that avoiding the risk was a poor bargain for our minter. She lost $9,000 by going into the market. True, but it is important to remember that she also had 100 ounces of gold to sell. When she finally sells those 100 ounces, presumably at $400 an ounce, she will be making a profit of $9,000 over what she had originally anticipated selling for (100 ounces at $310 equals $31,000; 100 ounces at $400 equals $40,000—profit is $9,000). She will have made back in the real market the $9,000 she lost in the futures market (roughly speaking). Basically, all that she was out was the broker's small commission. (In the real world it doesn't usually work out quite this precisely, but usually it comes close.) The speculator, unlike the hedger, however, buys *or sells* without having any need for the actual metal or having any gold to actually sell. This participant assumes the risk for the hedger and in return hopes to reap big profits.

The rules are the same for the speculator as for the hedger. The speculator can agree to buy or sell at some future date and simply put up a deposit now to open a contract. The speculator hopes to be able to eventually offset this contract with another and in between make a profit. Note that not only can the speculator enter the market without enough money to cover the full contract price, because of the deposit/margin, he or she can enter the market without any gold to sell!

When opening a buying contract, it is termed establishing a "long" position. When opening a selling contract (without metal) it is termed a "short" position.

At this point, some readers may be asking, how can someone sell gold they don't own? It doesn't seem logical.

Rest assured it is perfectly logical and it goes on all the time on the commodities markets. In fact, studies have shown that only about 3 to 4 percent of contracts ever involve actual delivery! That means that better than 95 percent of all contracts are in reality paper trades.

If you're confused about selling without actually owning the gold, let's try another example.

In a conventional transaction, the investor, hopefully, buys low and sells high to make a profit (as discussed in the last chapter). What is implied by this transaction is the element of time. It is assumed that the investor buys first, then time passes, and finally the investor sells. This time element is only an assumption. Why couldn't someone go the other direction in time? Why couldn't someone sell high and then buy low?

The reason, it might be argued, is that you must have the metal first in order to sell it. But, that's only true on the bullion market. In the futures market we're dealing in paper, not metal. In the futures market you don't have to have metal in your possession first, in order to sell it—you only need a paper contract. Therefore the constraint of metal ownership that applies to bullion sales does not apply to the futures market. It is, in fact, possible to first sell high and then, if the market works in your favor, buy low.

That's what is meant by selling short—selling a commodity you don't yet and may never own.

If it's still a blur, you can try reading up on the subject in pamphlets distributed by the commodity exchanges (see the end of the chapter). Talking with brokers can also prove helpful. But, if after doing all these things you still find it confusing, perhaps you should stick to buying and selling the actual metal.

This chapter is designed to just give the reader the flavor of the futures market so you can decide whether you should learn more about it. The reader should keep in mind, however, that we have barely skimmed the surface. We have not discussed the role of regulators or banks in the market. We have not gone into trading houses or floor traders. We have not gone into "spreads" and "straddles," nor the different types of market orders such as a "limit order," "open order," or a "day order." Nor have we covered hundreds of other elements.

It is not my intention to cover these items nor to overwhelm you with them. They are the fit subject for a book devoted exclusively to commodities futures. My intention here is only to mention them so that you will have some perspective on the vast amount of material that you may yet have to cover before you would want to seriously consider making your first futures investment.

Additional information

For booklets and more information on the subject of gold futures, the investor may want to contact several commodities exchanges directly:

Chicago Mercantile Exchange
International Monetary Market
444 W. Jackson Blvd.
Chicago, IL 60606

New York Mercantile Exchange
Dept. of Research and Education
Four World Trade Center
New York, NY 10048

Most commodity brokerage firms also offer a variety of booklets explaining the field.

7

Numismatic gold

The world of bullion gold is the most popular for most investors in the precious metal. But, is it necessarily the best way to invest in gold? There is another possibility which, for some investors, holds even greater rewards—"numismatic" gold.

The word "numismatic" simply means coin collector. "Numismatic gold" is a term which refers to gold coins which are bought for two distinct, but combined reasons. The first reason is the gold content of the coin itself. Investors buy numismatic gold just as they buy bullion gold—to get gold. The second reason is rarity. In a numismatic purchase the coin is valuable because there are very few of that denomination, date, mint, or whatever coin available. In other words, even if the coin contained no gold, it would still be worth more than the value stamped on its face. In a numismatically valuable gold coin, the price may be 40 percent or more higher than the bullion price for gold; that additional amount reflects numismatic value.

At this point the reader may be feeling some confusion. Didn't we earlier say that in order to make the best investment, one should consider buying as close as possible to the bullion price for gold? What about Harriet back in the introduction and her experiences with the gold bracelet? She lost money because she bought much higher than the bullion price.

There is a big difference between normal jewelry gold as an investment and numismatic gold. In jewelry gold the price added on to the bullion price may not be recoverable by the investor when it comes time to sell (assuming the price of gold stays constant). In numismatic gold, the added-on price is not only usually recoverable, but may increase. (We are, of course, not speaking of high-karat jewelry such as chains which may be sold very close to the bullion price for gold.)

A numismatic gold coin is a two factor investment. One factor is the gold itself. The other factor is the rarity of the piece.

Most typically, both factors go up at the same time. Let's take a hypothetical example. We're buying a U.S. gold eagle ($20) which contains just under 1 ounce of pure gold. The price of gold is $300 an ounce. What would we expect to pay for the coin? We might expect to pay close to $500 for the coin, depending on the year of issue and condition.

That $200 added-on cost was for its numismatic or rarity value. What happens when the price of gold goes to $400? What is the value of our double eagle?

In terms of gold content, it is close to $400. One would think that $400 plus the $200 numismatic value would raise the price to $600. However, in the past, many times, the numismatic value went up as well. Thus the coin might now actually be worth close to $670.

What this means to the investor is that not only has he or she made a $100 profit on the advance in gold price (from $300 an ounce to $400 an ounce), but also has made nearly $70 profit on the advance in numismatic value ($200 to $270). (Of course, this profit is offset by the fact that our investor had to pay more for the coin initially.)

In our example, we estimated the numismatic value of the coin to be roughly 40 percent of the price. When gold went up in

CHART 7A FIVE-YEAR COIN PRICE INDEX

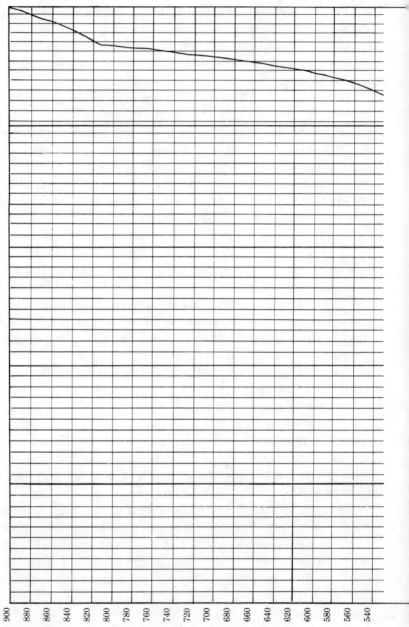

900 880 860 840 820 800 780 760 740 720 700 680 660 640 620 600 580 560 540

Courtesy of *COINage Magazine*.

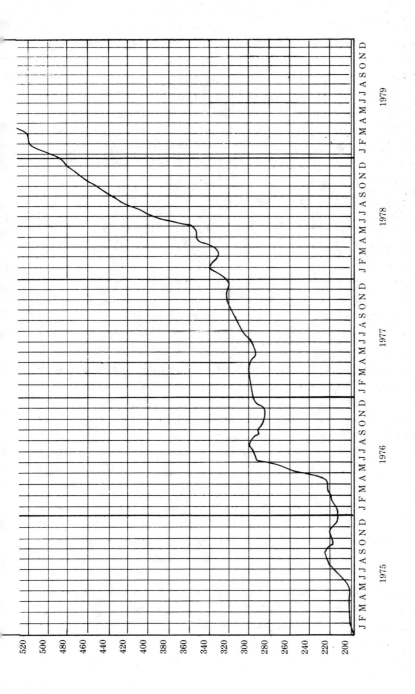

COINage Magazine's COINage Price Averages (CPA) indicating the direction in price of the coin market. The chart averages 20 key coins (listed below) each month from 1975 through late 1979. Note that the chart's left legend is an "index" and does not list coin prices. Also note that this chart is for coins in general, not specifically for gold coins. Gold coins in most cases, however, have done at least as well or better than this index indicates.

20 CPA KEY COINS

1909-S VDB Cent	1953-P Franklin Half
1960 SD Lincoln Cent	1955-P Franklin Half
1939-D Jefferson Nickel	1964-D Kennedy Half
1950-D Jefferson Nickel	1965 Kennedy Half
1916-D Mercury Dime	1921 Morgan Dollar
1921-P Mercury Dime	1921 Peace Dollar
1949-D Roosevelt Dime	1934-S Peace Dollar
1955-P Roosevelt Dime	1950 Proof Set
1932-D Washington Quarter	1955 Proof Set
1955-D Washington Quarter	1964 Proof Set

price, we *assumed* the numismatic value went up accordingly to maintain that 40 percent margin.

In the real world, while this sometimes happens, those factors which influence the price of gold are usually different from those which influence rarity. Therefore, the numismatic value of a gold coin may move more rapidly or slower than the price of gold. In some cases it may even move in the opposite direction from the gold content.

However, since, as the price of gold goes up, small investors begin buying more of it and since numismatic gold tends to be a small investor's market, both numismatic and bullion value tend to move in the same direction (though not always at the same rate).

In recent years many U.S. gold coins have appreciated far *quicker* in numismatic value than gold has moved in bullion value. And this is why many investors find them of great interest.

Numismatic coins in general over the last few years have

increased rapidly in price. The most graphic illustration I know
of the general advance of the coin field overall is the accompany-
ing chart presented through the courtesy of *COINage* magazine.
It lists the price of 20 *non-gold* coins on an index going back for
five years. Note the rapid price appreciation during the latest
years on the chart.

While the chart is for non-gold coins, gold coins themselves
depending on year and condition have tended to do as well or
better.

Scarcity

As we noted, price in this field is a function of scarcity and
scarcity is largely a function of how many of the coins are
available and what is their quality. (Another influence is popularity. A coin may be minted in great quantities, but because it
is popular, it is saved in extraordinary amounts, thereby making
it difficult to find and raising the price. The Kennedy half dollar
in its first years was an example of this.)

Mintage

The best clue we can have as to how many coins are available
or, to put it another way, how scarce is the coin, is to see how
many were originally minted. The U.S. Mint regularly provides
this information. (A handy source is *A Guidebook of U.S. Coins*,
by R. S. Yeoman, Whitman Publishers, which lists *all* U.S. coins
not only giving their mintage but their recent prices. The book
sells for under $5.) The number of coins minted varies from year
to year with some years having very high mintage, others very
low.

One might think that knowing how many coins were minted
would solve our problem with regard to scarcity. We could check
the records and see which years had the least coins minted.
These would be the scarcest and, therefore, the most valuable.

There is a problem. Coins eventually wear out and because of
this are taken from circulation. Knowing how many were

minted is not that big a help in knowing how many are still out there. However, by chance, we might assume that those with big mintages still had more in circulation than those with low mintages.

There is, however, a bigger problem. Bullion gold was called in by the government and melted down in 1933. This applied to nearly all U.S. gold coins. (Remember, at that time, they were considered circulating coinage just as dimes, nickels, and quarters are today.)

Vast quantities of gold coins were called in and melted into bars, perhaps most of those ever minted. Suddenly, with regard to gold coins, our mintage figures become undependable.

How, then, do we determine the scarcity of gold coins?

I have seen many studies that have attempted to do this. None, I believe, were satisfactory. What they have shown in general is that the latest issue gold coins, those in the late 1920s and early 1930s are the scarcest today. This stands to reason since those coins were considered to have virtually no numismatic value back in 1933 just as a 1980 dollar has little numismatic value today. They were probably the first melted. (They also had smaller mintages.) It would be hard, depending on condition, to find any gold double eagles ($20), for example, minted after 1929 that had a value of under $5,000 per coin today! Yet coins minted earlier might sell for only $500.

Ultimately, it is the marketplace which determines the scarcity and thereby the price of gold coins. Those coin years where few are offered for sale have higher prices. Those with many for sale have lower prices. The problem here, of course, is that some few people may be hoarding great quantities of the coins and may suddenly release them causing the price to plummet. This happened most recently when the U.S. government "found" some three million silver dollars of the 1800s and offered them for sale to the public.

Scarcity, therefore, particularly with U.S. gold coins is largely a matter of how scarce the coin is *at the time you buy or sell.* If it's in short supply, the price will be higher—in large supply, lower.

Condition

Another factor which determines the value of any numismatic coin is condition. When coins are struck at the mint, they are said to be in "mint condition." As they pass out into the world of commerce and circulation, they deteriorate. Each time they touch another coin or a finger rubs across them, some of the detailed image is lost. Their condition deteriorates. The American Numismatic Association has adopted a scale for noting the condition of coins, the "Official ANA Grading Standards for U.S. Coins" (Whitman Publishers).

A nearly perfect coin as it comes from the mint (without any mint scratches or marks) is considered "mint state" or "MS-70." As the coin deteriorates it goes down on the scale. Grades from MS-70 to MS-60 are considered "uncirculated" or never having touched human hands. Grades to "AU-50" are considered "about uncirculated." Through "EF-40" is "extremely fine"; through "VF-20," "very fine"; and down through "fine" and "good."

Most coins must be in the higher grades before they are considered numismatically valuable. For example, a 1925D $20 gold (the "D" stands for the Denver mint where it was struck), might be valued at $500 in Very Fine (VF-20) condition; $1,000 in Extremely Fine (EF-40) condition; or even $2,500 in Mint State (MS-60) condition. The price difference was $2,000 between the lowest and the highest condition.

Collectors are almost always interested in coins in the best condition. In recent years, therefore, the biggest price increases have occurred in the highest condition coins.

Therefore, if you're interested in a gold coin with strong numismatic value, you'll probably be looking for a high-priced piece in a high-quality condition. On the other hand, if numismatic value is of some consequence, but you're mainly after bullion value, you'll tend to stick with lower-priced gold coins in the lesser grades of condition.

Which offers the best opportunity for appreciation? My own personal observation is that coins with strong numismatic value have consistently outpaced coins bought just for the gold bullion value. This belief is shared by many coin dealers who buy and sell gold bullion coins largely as a means of getting potential customers in the door. Once inside, they present the possibilities of coins with strong numismatic value.

Which brings us to the matter of resale. As noted in Chapter 1, the premium paid on a bullion coin partly comes back to the investor at resale time. The actual cost to the investor, therefore, can be as low as 2 percent. Does the same hold true for gold coins with numismatic value?

Yes and no. As the coin has *less* numismatic value and greater bullion value, the mark-up by the dealer (difference between what you can buy and sell for) tends to be lower. (It probably, however, never gets as low as the 2 percent for bullion coins.)

On the other hand, as the numismatic value *increases*, so does the spread or mark-up. On coins with strong numismatic value the spread between what you can buy a coin for and sell it back for may be as high as 20 percent or more. While this may seem extraordinarily high, remember, there are relatively fewer buyers for the numismatically scarce coins and they are far harder to sell than bullion coins. That's why dealers can claim such a strong mark-up.

Many investors, however, gladly pay the higher mark-ups because they feel they are getting higher appreciation.

Making the investment decision

Should you invest in numismatic gold coins? Given the choice, I personally would pick numismatic coins, but I would be very selective about date and condition. Which means that buying numismatic involves more effort on the part of the investor. You have to become not only a gold expert, but a numismatic expert.

A final word here needs to be added regarding condition. NEVER try to grade the condition of any numismatic coin unless you're an expert. It is extremely difficult and is a job for someone who's had years of experience. What may look like a perfect coin to you may in actuality be a lesser grade. Therefore, if you're seriously considering entering the numismatic field, your best bet as a beginner is to buy cautiously and choose your dealer well. A good, reputable dealer will grade coins fairly. He or she will want your business not only when you buy, but when you sell. You won't be sold a coin as an MS-60 when you buy, then told it's only an AU-50 when it's time to sell, and offered half the price you think it's worth. Pick your dealer carefully— it can make or break your investment.

Rereading the section on counterfeits will also be helpful for numismatic coins are undoubtedly counterfeited more frequently than bullion coins. The American Numismatic Association provides a coin authentication service whereby it will tell you whether your coin is real or fake. The fees for the service are small. The A.N.A.'s address is:

American Numismatic Association
Colorado Springs, CO 80901

A good beginning book for those interested in learning more about collecting is:

High Profits from Rare Coin Investments
by Q. David Bowers
Bowers and Ruddy Galleries, subsidiary of General Mills
6922 Hollywood Blvd.
Los Angeles, CA 90028

For up-to-date information on coins:

COINage Magazine (about $10 annually)
17337 Ventura Blvd.
Encino, CA 91316

8

Gold coins
you can buy

This chapter is in reality more a list than a narrative. In it are given the major gold coins of the world which are usually purchased either for their numismatic or their bullion gold value. In some cases, of course, the coins are purchased for both.

The gold content and other figures for each coin were derived, when possible, directly from the mints. Although the list has been compiled from a variety of sources all of which are believed to be reliable, no warranty of accuracy is given or implied.

The calculations for gold content is given in both grams and troy ounces. They have frequently been rounded off to convenient decimals. For those readers who wish to make conversion calculations themselves, the following formulas will prove helpful:

Troy ounce   = 31.1035 grams

Gold content
in troy ounces = gold content in grams divided by (÷) 31.1035

Value of
  gold in coin = troy ounces of gold times (×) bullion price
               = troy ounces of total coin times (×) fineness times (×) bullion
                 price
               = total grams of coin divided by (÷) 31.1035 times (×) fineness
                 times (×) bullion price

A special thanks for the research and preparation of this listing goes to Clement F. Bailey, numismatic authority and writer. Without his aid it is doubtful the material could have been compiled within the time constraints imposed by book publishing.

Austria

1 ducat 3.5 grams gross weight (average), .9866 gold fineness, 20 millimeters in diameter, 3.45 grams of gold or .11095 of an ounce of gold.
4 ducat 14 grams gross weight (average), .9866 gold fineness, 35 millimeters in diameter, 13.8 grams of gold or .44381 of an ounce of gold.
4 gulden/or florins = 10 Francs 3.23 grams gross weight (average), .900 gold fineness, 19 millimeters in diameter, 2.90 grams of gold or .09346 of an ounce of gold.
8 gulden/or florins = 20 Francs 6.45 grams gross weight (average), .900 gold fineness, 21 millimeters in diameter, 5.805 grams of gold or .18663 of an ounce of gold.
10 corona 3.39 grams gross weight (average), .900 gold fineness, 19 millimeters in diameter, 3.051 grams of gold or .09809 of an ounce of gold.
20 corona 6.78 grams gross weight (average), .900 gold fineness, 21 millimeters in diameter, 6.102 grams of gold or .19618 of an ounce of gold.
100 corona 33.88 grams gross weight (average), .900 gold fineness, 37 millimeters in diameter, 30.49 grams of gold or .98033 of an ounce of gold.

It is important to understand that these seven bullion coins are not "originals." By that I mean that the original versions of these coins were struck principally in 1912 or 1915. Although these coins may carry those dates, they probably were struck much more recently.

Because they are restrikes, they are not usually considered legal tender coins. In fact, their main reason for existence is to be a bullion coin and to produce a profit for the Austrian Mint. They are sold at a premium (often between 9 and 15 percent) over the daily gold quote with the Austrian mint receiving a substantial portion of that money.

The pair of ducats, also found as dukat, are denominations that are steeped with history. The initial piece called the ducat is usually credited with its probable start in Sicily in the 12th century. Venice adopted the denomination in the next century and it has been an international piece of gold since that time. The term ducat is supposed to have been determined by the mention of such a piece in the motto found on the early issues.

The first ruler to issue the ducat did so without even knowing that it was a ducat. At least the first has been assumed, by many historians, to have been Roger II of Sicily, the Duke of Apulia, who ruled in the area of Sicily from 1095 to 1154.

He issued a coin with the Latin abbreviation, "SIT. T. XTE. D.Q.T.V.REG. IST. DUCAT," which, after complete translation into Latin and back to English means, "Unto thee, O Christ, be dedicated this Duchy which Thou rulest." The Latin for Duchy is Ducatus, but it was abbreviated on the coin as "DUCAT." Thus the name was created for the coin.

For many centuries many persons used the term "ducat" as one meaning coins or money with no thought that the silver or gold coin they held might be a ducat denomination.

In those days the gold ducat was a little larger in diameter than the present gold bullion coin but the other specifications have changed little in the past 362 years. Current ducat restrikes usually carry the 1915 date.

Modern day bullion coins with the name ducat are gold and the ducat is a gold denomination that has been used for five hundred years in Europe and other parts of the world. The modern ducat of Austria as a gold bullion coin, as well as the larger 4 ducat carry Emperor Franz Joseph I (1848–1916) on the obverse and the former double-headed eagle of the Holy Roman Empire on the reverse.

When the ducat was struck in Venice it was called the zecchino, with the figure of Christ on the obverse and the Doge of Venice on the reverse. The zecchino received its name from the Venice Mint or palace which was known as "La Zecca." The early pieces from Venice also carried the same Latin legend so the new one was called the "ducat." The Republic of Venice came to an end in 1797 and so did the gold zecchino, which no modern mint has continued as a gold bullion coin.

Austria has also restruck a pair of interesting denominations which would be the 4 and 8 florin coins which also have 10 and 20 francs associated with the issue.

The dual denominations are often called the 4 or 8 gulden pieces which is what the gold florin was known as in Austria, Hungary, as well as Germany. The name originally came from the German name for "golden penny" or Gulden Pfennig. The Austria issue was therefore a 4 gulden or florin coin or the higher 8 gulden or florin coin.

In addition to the florin or "Fl" on the coin the value in francs "Fr" is also noted. The French notation was used due to an agreement with the Latin Monetary Union.

The Latin Monetary Union was the name given to the alliance which was first formed in 1863 made up of France, Belgium, Italy, and Switzerland.

The idea of the Union was for each country to keep their individual denominations but to adopt a common regulation for the respective moneys. At the time there were twenty other countries interested in the Union and the representatives of those countries agreed to use the French franc as the basis for the uniform system.

The United States was represented and through the efforts of the members that attended the Union a couple of pattern coins were produced in copper and aluminum for a projected gold trade coin. The dual denominations on those issues were 5 Dollars, 25 Francs and one of 10 Florins, 25 Francs which was designed for use in trade with Austria. The United States Congress never passed the program so the pattern coins were left to tell the tale.

Austria, by a decree in March of 1870, struck the dual denominations to the specifications described above. The portrait of Franz Joseph I was again used on the obverse with the double headed eagle as the reverse design flanked by the dual denomination near the eagle's claws. The 1892 date is the normal one for present restrikes of the gold bullion coins.

The 3 corona denominations are also known by the English name of "crown." The new coin standards of Austria in 1892 listed the corona as the basic denomination with the minor denominations called the heller. In the decimal system 100 heller equalled 1 corona.

The three denominations being restruck in Austria carry the portrait of Franz Joseph on the obverse which is surrounded by the inscription, usual for the year of 1912 or 1915, which states "FRANC IOS. I. D. G. IMP. AVSTR. REX BOH. GAL. ILL. ETC. ET. AP. REX. HVNG." all of which carried the idea that "Francis Joseph I by the grace of God, Emperor of Austria, King of Bohemia, Galicia and Illyria, and King of Hungary" has issued the coin.

The reverse of the coins carry the double eagle with denomination and date in two places. One is over the eagle in Roman numerals while the second is in exergue or at the base of the design.

It has often been remarked that the rulers in Europe would have had to issue very huge coins in order to use all of the titles they claimed, even if abbreviated.

The Hapsburg rule came to an end in 1918 and the coin issues credited to Charles I or Karl I were so limited that it is claimed that only one example of a gold 20 corona coin exists which is in the national collection of Austria in Vienna. Others claim that several gold pieces exist but thus far only the one has been verified.

Other issues of Charles I were some 2 heller pieces and 20 heller denominations struck in iron but these were identical to the last issues of Francis Joseph but were dated 1918.

When Austria was declared a republic in 1918 it did not immediately strike coins but waited until 1923 for new coinage. This period of time, 1918–1923, gapped the time of the great inflation in Europe when new higher denominations of currency would be printed before the previous lower denominations had a chance to be used.

Belgium

20 francs   6.4516 grams gross weight, .900 gold fineness, 21 millimeters in diameter, 5.806 grams of gold or .1866 of an ounce of gold.

The 20-franc gold coin of Belgium is included in this listing, not because it was ever designed to be a gold bullion coin, but because the price of an ounce of gold has pushed the 1914 issue into the bullion field.

The issue of 20 francs produced by the Brussels Mint in 1914 was made in the same quantity for each of the official languages of the country, French and Flemish.

The Flemish inscription around the head of the King Albert is "Albert Koning Der Belgen," while the French is "Albert Roi Des Belges." The quantity currently listed is 125,000 pieces but that figure becomes highly questionable due to the quantity of 20-franc gold coins available as collector items.

The design of the coin was made by G. Devreese. King Albert evidently wore the Star of the Order of Leopold when he posed for the portrait as that is shown on the coin design.

The Star of the Order of Leopold was put into fact by King Leopold I in July of 1832 as a reward for services rendered to the country. The Order can be given to Belgians as well as foreigners for military, maritime, or civil service. Each of these divisions has five classes descending in importance.

Canada

Maple Leaf   1 ounce pure gold (.999 fine), 30 millimeters in diameter.

The introduction of the Maple Leaf gold bullion coin by Canada is their first entry into the area of gold bullion pieces. The Canadian coin carries the Maple Leaf of Canada on one side with the marks to identify it as a .999 fine gold 1-ounce coin. The opposite side has the portrait of Queen Elizabeth II as well as the denomination 50 dollars and the date of 1979.

The 1979 issue was struck in a quantity of 1 million with about half of that production being made available to the United States. The $50 (Canadian) value on the coin has no bearing upon the actual value of the piece. As with all bullion coins the daily gold quote on the free market in ounces will determine the actual value of the Maple Leaf.

The coin is being struck by the Royal Canadian Mint and has been made a legal tender piece by the Government of Canada. As a legal tender piece it will also be cataloged as a coin by other nations.

The master of the Royal Canadian Mint, Yvon Gariepy, told leaders of the Canadian gold mining industry, "We know that every coin we strike must reflect the dignity of Canada," as they observed the minting of the new Maple Leaf.

The 50-dollar denomination placed on the Maple Leaf was done in consultation with the Gold Committee of the Minting Association of Canada as well as advice from other countries who have issued gold bullion pieces.

Canada may be going after both worlds in the gold field, that of the investors as well as that of the numismatists. The low production of the 1979 issue, limited to 1 million coins, may be of great interest to pure collectors as well as investors. No bullion pieces with legal tender status have been collected by year date in the numismatic field before and this Maple Leaf may become the first.

OTHER CANADIAN GOLD COINS

Modern gold coins of Canada have enjoyed a unique niche with collectors as well as investors. Another coin, of 1967, issued as a 20-dollar gold coin for the Canadian Centennial was a popular coin in the United States as well as in Canada. Regardless of the restrictions placed on the owning of the coin by United States citizens, more than half of the production has been estimated as being in the hands of collectors south of the Canadian border, and many came out in the open as the restrictions of ownership were lifted.

The $100 gold coin struck for the Olympics by Canada in 1976 was made in two versions. One was a 14-karat gold coin which weighed 13.3 grams in a 27 millimeter diameter. The coin contained .5833 fine gold which when multiplied by the total weight of 13.3 grams amounted to one quarter of an ounce of gold in the piece. The second version of the coin, struck in "proof" (a special production technique for coins not generally made for circulation but for numismatic sale) had 22-karat gold content. The total weight was 16.9 grams in a 25 millimeter diameter, the gold content of the piece was one half an ounce. The restricted mintage of such pieces put them more in the rarity class rather than a speculator or investment classification.

The $100 (Canadian) gold coin of 1977 for Queen Elizabeth's 25th anniversary of the accession to the throne was made of silver and gold. The total weight of the coin was 16.5 grams with 91.6 percent gold (.916 fine gold) and 8.3 percent silver (.083 fine silver).

The gold content of the coin was slightly under half an ounce of gold but the mintage was low and the value as a rarity will probably exceed that of the gold market value.

The next gold coin produced by Canada was their $100 unity coin, so called because of the unity between the ten provinces and two territories of Canada. This gold coin had a total weight of 16.9 grams with a gold content of 91.6 percent or .916 fine gold. That made the gold content of the coin a full half ounce of gold. (All figures for calculations should be carried out to four places, but are only carried out to one place here for the sake of examples.)

Another happenstance occurred with the unity coin that made it very popular. The price of an ounce of gold increased and the original Canadian offer was made prior to the high price rise and the value of the gold in the coin was almost equalled by the price of an ounce of gold. The Canadian Mint was swamped with orders for the unity coin as a result. At the same time the Canadian postal strike was in progress and mail being sent to the Canadian Mint was not accepted by U.S. Post Offices. Many dealers hand-carried their orders to the Canadian Mint for the issue.

The last $100 gold coin issued by Canada prior to the Maple Leaf was the one for the International Year of the Child dated 1979. This coin also carries one half ounce of gold and was restricted in mintage which puts it into the numismatic field rather than pure gold bullion investment.

The previous experience with the $100 gold coins gave Canada the inspiration to enter the gold bullion market with the Maple Leaf. The Maple Leaf rather than being restricted to coin dealers or wholesalers is offered by selected banks, brokerage houses, and other similar types of investment companies.

Chile

20 peso 4.068 grams gross weight, .900 gold fineness, 18.5 millimeters in
diameter, 3.66 grams of gold or .1177 of an ounce of gold.
50 peso 10.1698 grams gross weight, .900 gold fineness, 24 millimeters in
diameter, 9.1528 grams of gold or .2942 of an ounce of gold.
100 peso 20.3396 grams gross weight, .900 gold fineness, 31 millimeters in
diameter, 18.3056 grams of gold or .5885 of an ounce of gold.

The three coins listed above are the smaller-sized pieces which were first
produced in 1926 and later. Some sources list the pieces as .9166 fine gold while
others seem to lean in the direction that the coins are made from .900 fine gold.
The .9166 fine gold pieces were produced in the 20 peso denomination prior to
1926.

Some very scarce dates exist in the 20 and 50 peso denominations with a great
amount of conjecture that they may still be in the vaults of the Central Bank of
Chile, which may or may not be a rumor.

The three coins are the same in appearance as to design with the only
noticeable differences being the size and denominations noted on the reverse.

The three denominations are also the only gold coins of Chile that will
probably be found in the bullion market or even as collector coins.

The interesting fact about the pieces is the double denomination on the
reverse. The 20 peso is listed as "Veinte peso" or "Dos condores" which means "20
pesos, 2 condores." The 50 peso is given as a 50 peso or 5 condores while the 100
peso is marked as such with the added 10 condores denomination.

The condores is taken from the condor, the bird that is so popular for most of
the Chile coinage.

In 1967 a series of gold bullion pieces were minted as commemorative issues.
The values were for 50, 100, 200, and 500 pesos and each commemorated a
different event. The issues were minted in a quantity of 12,000 for each
denomination and stand as collector gold pieces.

The Liberty on the three coins has been described as having a hairdo of the
coiled hair type as opposed to the previous issues which had Liberty as a draped
head. (It is certain that anyone who has anything to do with coiffures would not
really understand the language given to the various hairdos of the many
different Liberty images.) The head is surrounded by the name of the country
and the date is in exergue.

The reverses of the coins have the denomination at the top and bottom with the
country arms flanked on the left with the denomination and on the right with the
mint mark of Santiago.

Colombia

5 peso 7.9881 grams gross weight, .9166 gold fineness, 22 millimeters in
diameter, reeded edge, 7.321 grams of gold or .2354 of an ounce of gold.

The popular Colombia gold coin was made that way in the 1970s when great
quantities were placed on the market. It carries 23 percent of an ounce of gold

which is just one of the reasons for its popularity. The near quarter-ounce piece is not so expensive that the average investor cannot take part in the holding of a few pieces.

The design of the coin has Simon Bolivar, the South American liberator, on the obverse of the coin. Bolivar is considered the George Washington of several South American countries including Colombia. The name of the country surrounds the important portrait with a date under the bust, a date that is not necessarily the date of production of the coin. The most common date appears to be 1924.

The reverse carries the denomination, gross weight of the coin, fineness of the gold, and the Colombia coat-of-arms.

The coat-of-arms dates back to the days of Colombian independence from Spain, but it was adopted in 1832 and minor changes were made in the arms in 1948 and 1955.

The major device is a shield divided into three equal sections. The middle part of the shield displays the red cap of liberty. This cap dates back to ancient Rome to a point in time when slaves were given their freedom. As a sign that they were free men they started to wear the "pilevs," a special kind of cap with a long top that droops to one side. The French revived the idea in their revolution in the late 1700s and the cap also became part of the independence movement from Spain by the South Americans.

Above the red cap is a pomegranate (representing New Granada) flanked by cornucopias. One of the cornucopias is spilling coins and the other fruit. At the lower third of the shield the Atlantic and Pacific oceans are shown divided by the Isthmus of Panama (which at the time of the selection was part of Colombia). The condor holds up the shield by a laurel rope and the shield is backed by four national flags which were those of the rebels against Spain.

There are other, later issued, gold coins in very high denominations such as pieces with 100 pesos all the way to a 2,000-peso gold coin. These pieces, while interesting, are not really gold coins made for circulation nor are they gold coins made for the bullion market.

The limited production of the coins puts them in a collector classification and not in the true gold bullion classification.

Most of the pieces are commemoratives for a particular person or event that is of importance to Colombia. None of the total mintages went much higher than 25,000 and some went as low as 5,000 pieces.

Some of the coins were made to be sold or distributed in sets and hence the individual coins were never really made available to any market.

France

10 francs 3.2258 grams gross weight, .900 gold fineness, 19 millimeters in diameter, 2.903 grams of gold or .0933 of an ounce of gold.

20 francs 6.4516 grams gross weight, .900 gold fineness, 21 millimeters in diameter, 5.806 grams of gold or .1867 of an ounce of gold.

100 francs 32.2580 grams gross weight, .900 gold fineness, 35 millimeters in diameter, 29.032 grams of gold or .9334 of an ounce of gold.

100 francs 6.550 grams gross weight, .900 gold fineness, 21 millimeters in
diameter, 5.895 grams of gold or .1895 of an ounce of gold.

The four French gold coins mentioned above are listed for informational
purposes as the only coin struck in quantity in the list was the 20-franc coin.
That particular coin was restruck in the 1950s and probably later with dates of
the early 1900s.

The pair of 100-franc gold coins listed are of different sizes with the early date
(1874–1914) and in the size of 35 millimeters being the most popular and
probably the most readily available. The smaller 100-franc gold coin with the
dates of 1929 through 1936 is the scarcer of the two 100-franc coins as most of
the issue were melted. The devaluation in 1936 in France caused most of the
issue to go into the melting pot.

The 10-franc gold coin minted off and on from 1878 through 1915 is often
found in collections with few of them being made available as gold bullion
pieces. The design carried the head of Marianne on the issues of 1899 through
1915.

Marianne is the personification of the French Republic used as a coin design,
either as a head design or as a sower of grain. The story about the model usually
mentions how she was more interested in the money for the work than the fact
that she was to be used as a model for France.

The reverse of the 10 franc in question uses the design called the rooster which
is an actual misnomer as it is the "cock of Gaul."

The common 20-franc denomination in gold carries the same designs on the
obverse and reverse. The dates of 1900 to 1914 do not indicate the year of issue
but are probably restrikes. Many sources claim that only the dates from 1907 to
1914 are the restruck pieces while the others actually reflect the date of issue.

As with all restrikes there is no indication from the official mints involved as
to the use of which dates are on which denomination being restruck. This has
also hampered collectors as they usually wish to collect only coins that will
sometime rise in value due to the fact that the dates indicate the true mintage
year.

The large 100-franc gold coin (35 millimeters) shows an angel with the French
constitution and this is surrounded by the legend, "Republique Française." The
reverse carries the denomination in the center of the coin surrounded with the
famed French, "Liberte, Egalite, Fraternite."

France, from time to time, has witnessed a great number of official mints. In
fact they can be totaled to a sum of 20 different mints. Regardless of that fact
the great bulk of French coins have been minted at the French Mint in Paris
(moved in modern times to the new mint in the department of Gironde near
Pessac).

The gold francs mentioned above were originally struck in Paris as all of the
coins for the Second as well as the Third Republic of France were struck in
Paris. The mint mark of "A" as well as the marks of the mintmaster and assayer
appear on the coinage. The small design of the cornucopia and owl or other such
devices flank the "A" mint mark of Paris on the coins, although the small
designs are not restricted to those objects alone as the selection was up to the
individual involved.

The French gold coins in the 1800s influenced a great number of world gold coins because of the fact that the French pieces were selected as models by the Latin Monetary Union. The diameters of the French coins were standardized in other countries and one side effect was a standardization of jewelry holders for coins.

No one could mention the coins of France without mentioning Augustin Dupre whose designs have influenced the designs on French coins since his efforts in the late 1700s and early 1800s.

Augustin Dupre (August Dupre) was born in St. Etienne in 1748 and died in Armentieres in 1833. In between his work had been that of a genius.

Dupre was the son of a shoemaker who turned out to be a goldsmith and medalist. He started in the royal factory of arms while he studied sculpture and metal chasing. As usual with the youth of the time he made his way to Paris, for fame and fortune, at the age of twenty. His work as an engraver attracted the attention of the Spanish ambassador who then became a patron of Dupre which made it possible to set up a Dupre studio.

He became a master at engraving sword hilts as well as an engraver of dies for medals. It was at this time he became a Medalist of the Royal Academy of Painting as well as the assistant to the chief engraver of the French Mint. At the former French Mint building in Paris an alcove is devoted to Dupre for his work.

Dupre was a politician as well as an artist. He was appointed chief engraver of the French Mint at the time of the National Assembly rule in France in 1791. He held the job until 1803 when he was fired by Napoleon. His coin designs were used again in the 1870s by the Third Republic, almost forty years after Dupre died.

Franklin mint

One ounce   .999 fine gold, 34 millimeters in diameter.
Half ounce   .999 fine gold, 27 millimeters in diameter.
Quarter ounce   .999 fine gold, 21 millimeters in diameter.

The Franklin Mint, Franklin Center, Pennsylvania, a private mint not associated with any government function has produced three gold bullion pieces. They are properly called the Franklin Mint Gold Pieces and they come in three weights. The gold in the piece is not alloyed with any other material which appears to be the trend with current gold bullion pieces. Copper generally used as a hardener for coins is not used in this issue as the pieces are pure gold. This same idea is being used by the Canadian Mint with their Maple Leaf coin.

The price of the Franklin Mint Gold Pieces is based upon the daily quote for an ounce of gold, just as many gold bullion coins are priced. Added to this cost is the one that involves handling which may run about 4 to 5 percent.

The design of the new gold bullion pieces was supplied by Gilroy Roberts, the former chief sculptor-engraver of the United States Mint. The face or obverse side of each of the gold pieces carries the portrait of Benjamin Franklin with the inscription "The Franklin Mint" over the portrait and the current year of production, 1979, to the left of the face. Under the portrait is the listed weight of the piece in fine gold with the added notation that it is 24 karat .999 pure. The reverse portrays the distinctive sculpture of the American eagle as done by Roberts. The eagle is surrounded by thirteen stars. The famous stylized initials of Gilroy Roberts can be found on the truncated neck of Franklin on the obverse and to the left of the eagle's claws on the reverse.

Early in June of 1979 the Franklin Mint offered twenty-five hundred special proof editions of the three-piece issue to members of the Franklin Mint Gold Club. Each set of three gold bullion pieces, in proof, sold for $575 which, at the time, was only 30 percent over the bullion price of gold on the world market. The entire offer was sold out within weeks.

The non-proof bullion coins were first offered to the public in June of 1979. As already stated the price of the pieces is based on the daily quote of an ounce of gold. The initial distribution was made through selected banks, investment firms, as well as coin dealers through the country.

The success story of the Franklin Mint has been phenomenal since the day Joseph Segel, now retired, became the first Chairman of the Board of Directors of the National Commemorative Society in 1964.

Joseph Segel, a publishing executive, felt that many coin collectors were bored with their collections that offered little or no variety from year to year with the exception of the change of date and the variety of a mint mark. His idea was to form a commemorative society that would produce a monthly series of medals just for its membership. They would be commemoratives that would honor people, places, and events, an idea that was not really new to collectors and many of them laughed at the idea.

The Segel idea went further than the normal idea of production of mass medals to be sold to the membership of the society. He wanted to produce a proof medal of high quality similar to the European medallic artworks of times past.

The first NSC announcement in 1964 predicted that limited editions would gain collectors' interest as coin prices were driven upward.

The sterling-silver medals, in proof, were originally sold for $6.60 each and later increased to $7.25. The first medals were produced on contract with a firm in the Midwest. The quality desired and the security required by Segel forced him to search for a private mint which would do the proper job. The search did not turn up such a private mint and the next four medals were produced by a jewelry firm in New England.

Finally Segel organized the General Numismatics Corporation—which shortly became history as the Franklin Mint came into being—to strike the finest proof pieces that could be produced. At this time Gilroy Roberts resigned from his post at the United States Mint as chief sculptor-engraver and joined the new corporation. Roberts had gained fame at the United States Mint for his portrait of President Kennedy which appears on the half dollar. Eventually the Franklin Mint grew to a point where its annual income exceeded $20 million.

With the advent of the three gold pieces, tied to the price of an ounce of gold, the investor as well as the collector now has a choice of obtaining a small portion of gold—a quarter ounce, half ounce, or a full ounce of gold—by obtaining one of the Franklin Mint Gold Pieces.

The solid gold bullion pieces are still "art in medal form," as the pieces were designed to be the same size as the United States $20, $10, and $5 gold coins. This allows them to fit available jewelry mountings to be worn for beauty and treasured for value.

Great Britain

Sovereign (1 pound sterling) 7.9881 grams gross weight, .9166 gold fineness, .0833 copper, reeded edge, 22 millimeters in diameter, 7.3218 grams of gold or .2354 of an ounce of gold.

Half sovereign (1/2 pound sterling) 3.99405 grams gross weight, .9166 gold fineness, .0833 copper, reeded edge, 19 millimeters in diameter, 3.6609 grams of gold or .1177 of an ounce of gold.

The British sovereign or 1-pound coin has been a favorite of collectors for almost a hundred years. The small-sized sovereign was first minted in 1816 when Great Britain underwent a coinage specification change.

The sovereign and the half sovereign have had limited appeal to investors on the bullion market because of the difficulty of the mathematics required to determine the value of the gold in the piece according to any current gold ounce figure.

The gross weight of the coin times the fineness figure produces the gram weight of the gold in the coin. The gram weight divided by the number of grams in the troy ounce produces the decimal number of ounces in the coin. Multiply that by 100 and you rapidly have the percent of an ounce of gold.

The sovereign, as a respected coin on the market, does not have a great amount of gold and investment purchases often have been made in lots of 50, 100, or even 1,000 coins. The same applies to the smaller half sovereign which has exactly half as much gold as the 1-pound sovereign. The cost of handling the smaller lots overrides the advantage of small lot investment.

British sovereigns have been collected as real numismatic items as many of the yearly issues were not produced in great quantities. These pieces are purchased as individual coins and not in multiples. Most of the coins produced prior to World War II are collector coins with those dated after World War II being the gold bullion pieces.

The original gold coin of England was a project undertaken by Henry VII. He created a special commission to oversee the production of the first giant gold coin. The heroic-sized gold piece featured Henry VII seated on his throne. A seated king is usually called a "sovereign" and so the name was applied to the golden double ryal.

The image of Henry VII has him in a kingly robe seated on a kingly decorated throne with his crown on his head and holding an orb in his left hand and the sceptre of his office in his right hand. One oddity of the design is the incorporation of one of his favorite items, a portcullis, at the base of the design. (The portcullis is the iron grating with the sharp points which dropped shut at the gateway to a palace or castle.)

Eventually the coin was downgraded, and in 1816 the re-coinage produced the smaller sovereign gold coin. From that point forward only the head of the ruler graced the coin. Gone was the throne, the crown, the robes, and other bits of ruler paraphernalia including a lot of the original gold content.

The design of the reverse of the current bullion coins shows the slaying of the dragon by St. George. In the time of Queen Victoria (1837–1901) the reverse design displayed the Royal Arms.

Some of the original small-sized sovereigns carried the emblem of the Most Noble Order of the Garter. That is currently the highest award that can be given to the military or civilians. The garter is used in the design as a circle on the coin with the motto of the Order, "Honi Soit Qui Mal Y Pense," in French. In English it means or is generally considered to mean "Evil to him who evil thinks." You can find other translations but they usually have the same meaning.

The origin of the Order of the Garter took place in the time of Edward III (1327–1377). The romantic story has Edward III picking up a garter dropped by one of the noble ladies who had lost it on the floor at a court ball. The king put the garter on his leg and was supposed to have mentioned the French phrase. At any rate the Order of the Garter was founded in 1348 by King Edward III as a noble fraternity.

Saint George slaying the dragon on the sovereign reverse comes from a period of A.D. 300. A Christian soldier in the time of the Roman Empire was killed in the persecutions of those days. He was later adopted by the Crusaders as a guardian saint. King Edward III of England made him the patron saint of England. His killing the dragon dates back to other days as the heathens likened him to a dragon slayer.

The design of St. George taking care of his dragon was originally intended as a cameo by the artist Benedetto Pistrucci. Later on we find that Pistrucci became the chief engraver of the Royal Mint in London in 1817 and chief medalist in 1828.

The first St. George uses a broken lance to fight the dragon but later designs have him armed with a short sword. In either event he seems to have accomplished the task.

The current gold bullion sovereign is struck at the Royal Mint in England but is not usually listed in any of the coinage lists as the coin is not granted the cover of "legal tender."

Great Britain decided not to produce the gold sovereign any more at some point after World War II. The start of the new gold bullion sovereigns was determined by the widespread counterfeiting of the gold coin.

Much of this was due to the use of the sovereign in the Middle East as a trade coin. When it was no longer minted by Great Britain the void was filled by counterfeit gold pieces. Many of the gold coins were of the exact specifications of the original and were also struck (as opposed to cast). Struck pieces from dies makes it difficult to detect counterfeits unless one is an expert in genuine gold sovereigns. Gold was freely available after World War II and a great many of the counterfeits apparently came out of Italy. In most cases, as mentioned, the strikes were expert and the gold was genuine.

To protect themselves from a flooding market of fakes, the British government went back to the production of the sovereign. It is not used internally but is sold to world markets for a gold bullion coin.

The half sovereign is not currently produced but a great number which were made in previous years appear on the bullion market.

In the half sovereign designs you would be hard pressed to find any with Queen Elizabeth II or her father King George VI. Most designs will be those of Queen Victoria, King Edward VII, and King George V, which span the dates of the late 1800s to early 1900s. The reverse design is the same as those of the sovereigns, the obverse with the ruler and the reverse with the Royal Arms on some of the Queen Victoria issues and St. George slaying the dragon on the rest of the issues.

The sovereign denominations have not been restricted to the Royal Mint in England but they have been produced in the mints in Australia, India, South Africa, as well as Canada.

Specifications have been so precise on the sovereign that even the thickness is specified as 1.63 millimeters (which may represent an average of hundreds of struck pieces). The reeding on the edge (at least for the 1960s-dated pieces) is listed at approximately 105 serrations which are 7½ thousandths of an inch deep. The four million sovereigns struck in 1975 carried the date of 1974 and were designed for the gold bullion market. Thus far Great Britain has not restruck sovereigns, using the older dies and older dates for the issues.

Hungary

1 ducat 3.491 grams gross weight, .9866 gold fineness, 20 millimeters in diameter, 3.444 grams of gold or .1107 of an ounce of gold.

4 florint = 10 francs 3.225 grams gross weight, .900 gold fineness, 19 millimeters in diameter, 2.902 grams of gold or .0933 of an ounce of gold.

8 florint = 20 francs 6.45 grams gross weight, .900 gold fineness, 21 millimeters in diameter, 5.805 grams of gold or .1866 of an ounce of gold.

10 korona 3.387 grams gross weight, .900 gold fineness, 19 millimeters in diameter, 3.048 grams of gold or .0980 of an ounce of gold.

20 korona 6.775 grams gross weight, .900 gold fineness, 21 millimeters in diameter, 6.0975 grams of gold or .1960 of an ounce of gold.

100 korona 23.875 grams gross weight, .900 gold fineness, 37 millimeters in diameter, 21.4875 grams of gold or .6908 of an ounce of gold.

There are other gold coins that could be listed under Hungary but most of the rest are not really used for circulation nor are they made in large enough quantities to be classed as gold bullion investment pieces. They range in denomination from 50 florints (florins) to 1,000 florints.

Hungary was part of the Austro-Hungarian dual monarchy (Austrian emperor was also the king of Hungary). Many of the Hungarian gold coins have the same image of the Austrian Emperor on their coins as do the Austrian issues. The only difference is the legend which is in Hungarian. The reverse of the Hungarian coins carries the Hungarian arms instead of the famed double eagle of Austria.

For the most part the legends in Hungarian around the portrait of Francis Joseph are usually of this type, "Ferencz Joszef I K A CS ES M H S D O AP KIR," meaning "Francis Joseph, by the grace of God, Emperor of Austria and Apostolic King of the lands of Hungary, Croatia, Slavonia, and Dalmatia."

The normal reverse of the coins in question usually display the arms of Hungary supported by angels or some other variation of the arms.

The coat-of-arms of Hungary displayed on the golden coins of the issues involved dates back to about 1200. The official heraldic description has eight bands covering a shield completed by "red and gold" meaning the alternate colors of red and gold on the stripes. The whole is crowned by a Hungarian crown.

The famous Hungarian crown of St. Stephen actually is two crowns and is also a national relic of the Magyars. King Stephen I is supposed to have received a crown of two hoops and a cap consisting of thin sheet gold from Pope Sylvester III when he was converted to Christianity in the year 1000. The second crown called Greek or Byzantine consists of a circlet with ornaments with the back set in pearls. This was received from the East Roman Emperor Dukas in early 1700. The cross on top of the crown is a later addition and in each case is shown tilted, due to careless attachment.

Another famous crown is the one which was received by King Andreas from Emperor Monomachos as a present, in the 11th century. In the 1800s parts of the crown were plowed up in a field, a mystery for the piece.

On the coins of the 1800s and the restrikes being made of the gold issues, the old type Hungarian arms are to be found. In 1949 these old arms were replaced with a State emblem of Soviet design; after the revolt in 1956 a new State emblem was devised.

The 1 ducat coin described has 11 percent of an ounce of gold and is an official restrike by Hungary. The Hungarian gold coins may be marked as restrikes or they may not carry the identification. On many of the pieces they have placed a UP (uj penzveres) to indicate the piece is a Hungarian new strike or restrike. In some cases they have not used the UP but in those cases they have left off the mint mark for Budapest, the BP initials.

Confusion is probably the key word for coin collectors in trying to keep up with the restrikes as opposed to the original strikes.

In the bullion market it makes little difference about mint marks, restrike marks, or even coin dates, as long as the gold is authentic.

The 1 ducat has a rich gold fineness figure of .9866 which makes it more desirable to some purchasers. An interesting item about the 1 ducat is the fact that the restrikes will probably be dated 1870 but back in 1870 they did not mint a 1-ducat gold coin.

As in Austria the Hungarians struck coins to conform to the Latin Monetary Union. As the gold denomination of France was selected it is not surprising to find the Hungarian 4 or 8 florints mixed with the French franc denomination, both displayed on the reverse of the dual denomination coin. That was the reason for the initial issue and gold bullion was the reason for the restrikes.

The 10, 20, and 100 korona or kronen coins have also been restruck for gold bullion purchasers. Most of the restrikes are dated 1892 or 1898 for the 10 korona issues. The 20 korona have been observed with the dates of 1892 or 1895 as restrikes. The 100-korona coins have been restruck with the dates of 1892 and 1898, as well as the 100-korona commemorative of 1907.

The 1907 commemorative as a 100-korona denomination was issued initially for the 40th year of Francis Joseph's reign.

The restrike of this coin was supposed to have been limited to a small number but it is suspected that more may have been produced. There is no way to make the determination but the restrikes are supposed to have the small UP next to the date; pieces that do not have the mark are then considered to be originals struck in 1907. Those would be the collector coins while the marked issues would be the gold bullion pieces. The restrikes kept the U.S. Office of Gold and Silver Operations busy in the time when citizens of the United States could not hold bullion.

Hungary has also issued a complete series of gold coins starting with the People's Republic, with 1961 issues, followed by issues in 1966, 1967, as well as 1968. Those gold issues were as small as 50 florints and as high as 1,000 florints. They have been classed as collector pieces because of the small number of coins produced for each of the designs and denominations. Several of the pieces have a gold fineness of .986 which was the standard of the gold ducat first made in 1280 and continuing as a gold bullion coin.

India

5 *rupees* 3.887 grams gross weight, .9166 gold fineness, 18 millimeters in diameter, 3.562 grams of gold or .1145 of an ounce of gold.

10 *rupees* 7.774 grams gross weight, .9166 gold fineness, 22.5 millimeters in diameter, 7.125 grams of gold or .2290 of an ounce of gold.

15 *rupees* 7.988 grams gross weight, .9166 gold fineness, 22 millimeters in diameter, 7.32 grams of gold or .2354 of an ounce of gold.

1 *mohur* 11.66 grams gross weight, .9166 gold fineness, 25 millimeters in diameter prior to 1862, 24 millimeters in diameter after 1862, 10.68 grams of gold or .3436 of an ounce of gold.

2 *mohur* 23.32 grams gross weight, .9166 gold fineness, 32 millimeters in diameter, 21.37 grams of gold or .6872 of an ounce of gold.

Sovereign (British 1 pound) 7.988 grams gross weight, .9166 gold fineness, 22 millimeters in diameter, 7.32 grams of gold or .2354 of an ounce of gold.

India is one of the more difficult nations to analyze as they have restruck all of the British gold coin issues from the 1800s. The pieces were originally struck at the time India was part of the British Empire.

The extent of the coinage of India would fill several volumes as the coinage of the British and coinage of the native states were sometimes produced at the same time, with or without similarity of design.

The East India Company with the formal title of United East India Company issued a great number of coins for India as it was the real ruler of India rather than the British government. (The India mutiny of 1857 caused the transfer of power to the British crown.)

Restrikes of the East India Company 1- and 2-mohur gold coins have been extensive. They featured the portrait of William IV (1830–1837) of England with the inscription "William IIII, King," around the head and the date in exergue. The reverse of the design for both of the mohur denominations carried the lion design of England in front of a palm tree. East India Company appears around the top, denomination under the lion design in English as well as a native dialect.

The restrike program of India through the mints in Bombay and Calcutta has been done by customer order for these British gold coins. The sovereigns shown on the restrikes have been William IV, Queen Victoria, and George V. As Victoria had a very long reign (1837–1901) it would be normal to find a great number of restrikes with her image.

The first of the issues show the queen when she was young and her title on the coinage is "Victoria Queen" with the date. The reverse of the early issues dated 1841 have the same design as that of William IV.

In 1862 an older crowned queen is shown on the gold coins with the date of original issue on the reverse under the listed denomination of 1 mohur, 5 or 10 rupees. The dates run from 1862 to 1870.

A similar design was made later in 1870 with a fuller-faced queen but with the same design as previous issues with the reverse the same as above, denomination and date in the center surrounded by an ornate design.

The 1 mohur and 5 rupees of 1877 changed the title of Victoria from Queen to Empress but otherwise the designs remained the same.

The 1879 issues of gold were the 5 and 10 rupee coins with the title of Empress but with a fat face. With that gold issue the Victoria coins came to an end in India.

The last gold issue listed for British India was that of George V (1910–1936) in the 15 rupee denomination. The crowned, robed king is surrounded by the title of "George V King Emperor" on the face of the coin. The denomination and date are on the reverse with an ornate design around the information.

The British sovereign or 1-pound gold piece was also minted in India. It is the same type as the regular British sovereign with the exception that the mint mark for India is on the ground under the horse of St. George on the reverse, as a capital I. The full description of the coin can be found under the listing for Great Britain.

There are many private banks issuing gold bars, scalloped, square, round, or other sizes of gold pieces currently in India. The mark used for weight is the tola which is equal to 11.5 grams. As the tola is really a weight and not a denomination the pieces belong in the category of gold bullion bars or ingots. The division can be found as low as ¼ and ½ of a tola.

While mentioning the divisions of the tola we should also mention that the coins of the mohur denomination can be found in ⅛, ¹⁄₁₆, or ¹⁄₃₂ of a mohur as well as higher fractional pieces from ¼ to ½ mohur. All are in proportion to the 1-mohur gold piece.

Importance of the fractional gold pieces is uppermost when gold bullion rises in great value. The fractional bits are then available to those who do not have the money to purchase full-ounce bars or coins.

Indians are traditionally a gold-saving people as they fix the owning of gold higher in esteem than they do other materials or other currencies.

For collectors of coins the native states of India offer a great variety of gold pieces, which may or may not be restrikes, but which are made from genuine gold.

The genuine collector value of any British gold coins originally issued in India has dropped because of the restrikes being made. At the same time it should be mentioned that those purchasing gold pieces from India do so at bullion values or close to bullion values as older-dated pieces are not genuine oldies.

No one would mention India without the notation about the world's largest known gold coin. The coin was a 200-mohur gold coin struck in Hindustan in the reign of Shah Jahan.

Shah Jahan may not be as familiar as the edifice that was produced in his reign—the Taj Mahall at Agra for his favorite wife who was Arjumand Banu. She was better known as Mumtaz Mahall, "the distinguished one, of the palace."

Shah Jahan was born in 1592 and died in prison in 1666 after he was deposed by his son. He was the fifth emperor of Hindustan and the gold coin was made in the later days of his reign in 1654. The coin was 5⅜ inches in diameter and weighed approximately 70 to 74 troy ounces! If the coin was made from .9166 fine gold then the gold weight would be in the neighborhood of 67 troy ounces or 5.6 troy pounds of gold. Based on the ounce price of gold at $440 (one peak price in 1979) the coin would have a gold bullion value of about $28,000 to $30,000.

The coin disappeared, probably melted, in India in the 1818 to 1820 period of time. The only reason the coin is known is due to a casting of the piece held by the British Museum.

Liechtenstein

1 dukat (ducat)   3.49 grams gross weight, .986 gold fineness, 23 millimeters in
   diameter, 3.441 grams of gold or .1106 of an ounce of gold.
1 gulden taler (gold thaler)   10 grams gross weight, .986 gold fineness, 23
   millimeters flat to flat on a "klippe" or square planchet, 9.86 grams of gold
   or .317 of an ounce of gold.
1 vereinstaler (convention thaler)   29.5 grams gross weight, .900 gold fineness, 33
   millimeters in diameter, 26.55 grams of gold or .8536 of an ounce of gold.
10 dukat (ducat)   34.9 grams gross weight, .986 gold fineness, 43 millimeters in
   diameter, 34.41 grams of gold or 1.106 ounces of gold.

The four denominations listed above as issues from Liechtenstein are restrikes authorized by the authorities in Liechtenstein in 1966. They are gold bullion coins in the true sense of the word and they also protect the original issues by the inclusion of the letter "M" on the restrike. The "M" indicates that the pieces were restruck in the mint in Munich, Germany.

The 1 ducat or dukat appears with three different older dates as they carry the portraits of three different former princes of Liechtenstein, a country that is described as being 61, 62, or 65 square miles in size depending upon the source and date of reference.

The ducat of Prince Joseph John Adam was originally issued in 1728 in his reign as prince from 1721-1732. The second restrike was that of Prince Joseph Wenzel who ruled from 1748 to 1772 and the date of the original issue being restruck is 1758. The third ducat coin was that of Francis Joseph who ruled from 1772 to 1781 and the restrike is that of 1778.

In each case the prince is shown on the obverse with the coat-of-arms on the reverse. The country at the time of the original issue was part of the Holy Roman Empire.

The golden thaler was also restruck under the restrike program in 1966. This particular coin was originally struck as a gold ducat in the reign of Prince

Charles (1614-1627). The restrike has been produced on a square planchet of gold with the planchet being treated as a diamond shape in order to see the reproduction of the coin right side up.

The convention thaler produced in 1862 in gold was also restruck by the 1966 authority. This piece carries the image of Prince John II who ruled from the time he was eighteen in 1858 to his last year in 1929. In the time of Prince John II the country became an independent state but with close ties to Austria. Independence came in 1866 and in 1868 they abolished their army and remained neutral in all wars since that time. The reverse of the coin carries the arms of Liechtenstein.

The last two coins struck under the 1966 law are 10-ducat pieces. One was originally produced in 1616 in the reign of Prince Charles and the other was minted in 1728 under the authority of Prince Joseph John Adam. Both of the pieces carry more than an ounce of gold but are not as heavy in gold weight as is the Mexico 50-peso gold coin.

Modern gold coins also are being minted for Liechtenstein in the 10-, 20-, 25-, 50-, and 100-franc denominations. None of them have been designed for the gold bullion market and so they would be more properly listed in numismatic catalogs as collector items.

The country adopted the Swiss franc standard as the basis for its currency in 1924 and they followed the new Swiss law of 1952 in regards to their current money.

The principality was created by Emperor Charles VI of the Holy Roman Empire in 1719. In the early history of the area the princes named seldom visited their principality but were highly active in the cause of the Hapsburgs, which explains the close tie of Liechtenstein to Austria in its early history.

In current times Liechtenstein has become a headquarters for many international companies due to the low taxes of the state. It is currently headed by Prince Franz Josef II who was born in 1906 and who took the high post in 1938. A coin issue has been made by Liechtenstein in gold in three denominations (25, 50, and 100 franc) with the conjoined heads of Prince Franz Josef II and Princess Gina. The 100-franc denomination was minted in 1952 and the other two minted in 1956.

The flag of Liechtenstein also has an interesting design feature. Two flags are used with the use depending upon the way the flag is hung.

The design of the flag has two large stripes, blue over red, with a crown in the left top portion of the blue stripe. The head of the crown is always placed so that the top is pointing upward. That makes it necessary to have a flag for horizontal display and another for vertical display.

Mexico

2 peso   1.66 grams gross weight, .900 gold fineness, .100 copper, reeded edge, 13 millimeters in diameter, 1.494 grams or .04 of an ounce of gold.

2½ peso   2.083 grams gross weight, .900 gold fineness, .100 copper, reeded edge, 15.5 millimeters in diameter, 1.8747 grams or .06 of an ounce of gold.

5 peso   4.166 grams gross weight, .900 gold fineness, .100 copper, lettered edge, 19 millimeters in diameter, 3.7494 grams or .1206 of an ounce of gold.

10 peso 8.33 grams gross weight, .900 gold fineness, .100 copper, lettered edge,
   22.5 millimeters in diameter, 7.497 grams or .2411 of an ounce of gold.
20 peso 16.66 grams gross weight, .900 gold fineness, .100 copper, lettered edge,
   27.5 millimeters in diameter, 14.994 grams or .48 of an ounce of gold.
50 peso 41.66 grams gross weight, .900 gold fineness, .100 copper, lettered edge,
   37 millimeters in diameter, 1.2056 ounces of gold.

The above coins are currently available on the gold coin bullion market. The most popular coins of the six specified are the 50 peso and the 20 peso. Even so, all of the Mexican bullion pieces create interest for seekers of bullion coins.

The smallest gold coin in the set of six is the small 13-millimeter piece with its .04 ounces of gold (4 percent of an ounce) and marked as a 2-peso coin. The marking on the coin was first placed on the piece with the issue of 1918 and the issue was sporadic in the following years. The current gold bullion issues, when available, were probably minted within the past twenty-five years but with the date of 1945 as the pieces are restrikes by the Mexican government to be sold as gold bullion coins, as are the others in the Mexican series. The eagle design was popular in the era when the coin was first minted and that is the design on the obverse of the coin. The reverse gives the denomination, "Dos Pesos," within a wreath and the date displayed over the legend. In 1978 there were 460,000 pieces minted, probably with the 1945 date.

The 2½-peso gold coin was also first issued in 1918 and the yearly issues were not always made. The eagle of Mexico surrounded by United States of Mexico, in Mexican is the obverse of the coin. The reverse carries the head of Father Miguel Hidalgo with the denomination notation of "Dos Medio Pesos," and date. The 2½ peso is only 2½ millimeters larger in diameter than the 2-peso coin and it only carries 2 percent of an ounce more of gold than the 2-peso coin. The Mexico Mint in Mexico City struck 193,000 pieces in 1978 with the date assumed to be 1945. There are a few dates that have a little more value than the gold bullion in the coin due to the smaller mintage figures.

In 1905 the original issue of the 5 peso was made and once again the eagle is on the obverse with Father Hidalgo on the reverse. This is the first of the peso denominations to have the lettered edge of Independencia Y Libertad— Independence and Liberty. All of the higher peso denominations carry the same notation on the edge of the coin. As for pure numismatic coins, that is a questionable item but no such item would appear on the gold bullion market. In 1978 the reported mintage of the 5-peso piece was 105,000 pieces and probably with the restrike date of 1955.

Father Hidalgo was placed on the 10-peso gold coin of Mexico in the same year in which he graced the 5 peso, 1905. These were the first coins of the Republic of Mexico to carry the patriot. The design of the two gold coins is the same only the diameters and gold content differ (see specifications). At the present time it appears as though the 1905 issue is the only one that may be classed as a numismatic coin as a quantity of less than 20,000 were minted the first year of issue. Only eight dates are known to exist in the series and the 1959 date is the restrike date used on the current issues from Mexico for bullion purposes. The mintage figures of 1978 show a low quantity of 2,000 but they are probably 1959 dated.

The 20-peso gold coin of Mexico is interesting, not only for its 48 percent of an ounce of gold, but for the design. It carries the usual devices on the obverse for Mexican coins but on the reverse there is a difference. The use of the Aztec calendar stone for the design makes the coin a conversation piece, a collector item, and an excellent gold bullion coin.

The original stone was not really a calendar stone but received its name from the ring of the twenty day symbols around the head of the Sun God in the center of the stone.

Between the 1500s and the late 1700s the huge stone was missing. The calendar stone weighs several tons, has a twelve-foot diameter and a three-foot thickness and it seems impossible to have lost it. The Spanish when they ruined the temple to the Sun God threw out the stone. It was then found a few hundred years later buried in a street in Mexico City. It has since found a new home at the National Museum of Anthropology in Mexico City, another Aztec memento.

The 20-peso gold coin was originally struck in 1917 and the issue was not struck every year to its final end; in fact only six different dates can be counted for the issue from 1917 to 1959. The restrikes being made in Mexico appear to have 1959 dates on all coins regardless of the year of production.

In Mexico all gold coins went out of circulation or general use in the early 1930s which means that any pieces struck after World War II (1945) would be gold bullion pieces. The 20 peso is not recorded as being produced in 1978 for the bullion market.

The Mexico 50-peso gold coin is one of the heaviest and carries the largest portion of gold in regard to other gold bullion pieces. For that reason the 50 peso is a most popular coin with investors as it carries 1.2 ounces of gold.

The current 50-peso restrike carries on the obverse the eagle of Mexico surrounded by the United States of Mexico in the Mexican "Estados Unidos Mexicanos." The famed winged victory takes up the reverse flanked by the denomination and the fineness of the gold in the coin. Dual dates are also shown in exergue. The 1821 date found on the piece is in reference to the date of independence from Spain, the modern date is just a representative date as it has no recording factor in the march of coin dates.

The only popular name of the series of Mexico gold bullion coins is the one for the 50 peso which is "Centenario" or Centennial as the first of the series was struck in 1921 on the 100th anniversary of the independence day. It is a non-commercial coin that is widely purchased for its bullion content.

One of the odd issues of the 50-peso gold coin was minted in 1943. That issue was a genuine gold bullion piece as it did not carry the denomination on the coin. That was the style of the Krugerrand when it first came out in 1967 and one of the factors that has made the South African coin such a popular item. The current 50-peso restrike carries the denomination as well as the 1947 date.

One of the most confusing facets about the coins of Mexico, gold bullion pieces, or numismatic coins is the one that involves the nomenclature of obverse and reverse or the more popular "heads" and "tails" of the coin.

The Mexican coins were first cataloged by the portraits found on the pieces and that side was then called the obverse with the reverse of the coin normally displaying the eagle of Mexico and the name of the country.

Over the years that system has changed and the current proper designations have the eagle of Mexico with the surrounding country name as the obverse. This makes the "head" side of the coin actually the reverse or "tail." In any event catalogs can be found which treat the obverse and reverse differently.

Netherlands and Netherlands East Indies

1 ducat 3.49 grams gross weight, .983 gold fineness, 20.5 millimeters in
diameter, 3.43 grams of gold or .1102 of an ounce of gold.

This ducat carries a modern date but is of the same design as age-old ducats used a couple of hundred years ago. The armed knight is still gracing the obverse with the legend, "Gold Money for the Belgian Kingdom by Imperial Law," on a square design on the reverse. Some interpretations of the Latin "Belgii" on the reverse claim that it means "the Netherlands," and not Belgium. According to most observers the question is of no importance as the Netherlands struck the current issues.

Another small factor in the description of the coin is the fact that the current ducat is just a shade off from the original ducat gold fineness. The original ducat was specified as having .986 gold fineness but this piece apparently has a .983 gold fineness.

The coin is considered to be a trade coin or a gold bullion piece as it mingled with the sovereign of the British and the French 20-franc denomination in the Middle East and Asia where the confidence of the local money is not of the highest esteem.

The production of counterfeit gold coins in the area when the official issues were not minted caused the official issues to be minted again.

(The premium value for gold coins is collectible on every coin sold as opposed to a small premium for a large bar of gold. Minting coins from gold bars is a lot more profitable than just selling gold bullion in bar form as noted earlier.)

In the years prior to the entry of the U.S. citizen into the gold market, being restricted by law, the gold bugs of Europe bought and sold gold bullion pieces in the great marketplaces of Switzerland and Germany. These gold bullion pieces are now being found in the U.S. due to the gold bullion demand.

As the price of an ounce of gold goes higher and higher the smaller gold bullion coins will be in demand as their gold content doesn't make the cost of the piece a king's ransom.

If any gold bullion coin is offered as a proof coin then it can be immediately determined that the coin is being sold for a premium for collector purposes.

The Netherland gold ducat was made for the East Indies as a circulating gold coin up to the World War II era.

Peru

1/5 libra 1.5976 grams gross weight, .9166 gold fineness, 14 millimeters in
diameter, 1.464 grams of gold or .047 of an ounce of gold.

1/2 libra 3.994 grams gross weight, .9166 gold fineness, 19 millimeters in diameter, 3.66 grams of gold or .1177 of an ounce of gold.

1 libra 7.988 grams gross weight, .9166 gold fineness, 22 millimeters in diameter, 7.3218 grams of gold or .2354 of an ounce of gold.

5 soles 2.34 grams gross weight, .900 gold fineness, 15 millimeters in diameter, 2.106 grams of gold or .0677 of an ounce of gold.

10 soles 4.68 grams gross weight, .900 gold fineness, 18 millimeters in diameter, 4.212 grams of gold or .1354 of an ounce of gold.

20 soles 9.362 grams gross weight, .900 gold fineness, 23 millimeters in diameter, 8.425 grams of gold or .2708 of an ounce of gold.

50 soles 23.403 grams gross weight, .900 gold fineness, 29.5 millimeters in diameter, 21.062 grams of gold or .6771 of an ounce of gold.

100 soles 46.807 grams gross weight, .900 gold fineness, 36.5 millimeters in diameter, 42.126 grams of gold or 1.354 ounces of gold.

The gold coins listed above are gold bullion pieces made by Peru for the gold bullion market. Gold coins in Peru after 1950 were no longer considered to be legal tender coins. The dates of the issues listed above will all be from 1950 to a later date.

One of the gold bullion pieces also was issued which was in the 50-soles denomination but which was heavier in gross weight as well as gold content. That would be the 50 soles with a portrait of the first Lord Inca, Manco Capac.

All of the land, animals, and gold belonged to the Lord Inca in the Inca world. Thus the design of the 50-soles coin depicts the Lord Inca in a gold headdress as well as wearing a gold earring. The name of the country surrounds with date under the head. This heavy 50-soles coin stated on the coin as 33.436 grams with .900 fine gold, was made in 1930 and 1931 and once again in 1967 and probably through the 1970s.

The reverse of the coin is an Indian totem pole with the denomination across the top with weight and fineness of the coin circled below the design.

The obverse of the sole pieces displays a seated Liberty with a staff in her left hand and the freedom cap on top the staff. She is also holding a shield in her right hand. The denomination, weight, and gold fineness surround the design with the date in exergue.

On the reverse of the five coins is found the coat-of-arms of Peru with weight and fineness as well as the mark of the Lima, Peru, Mint—which is the word Lima.

The arms of Peru have been used on their coins from time to time and may vary slightly over the years. The empire of the Incas in Peru came to an end through the efforts of Francisco Pizarro and Peru stayed under the rule of Spain for nearly three hundred years. Peru was the last of the South American countries to gain independence from Spain.

The coat-of-arms was adopted in 1825 after independence was gained in 1821. The shield is divided into three sections with a llama in the first section, a tree described as a cinchona tree in the second section, and under it all is a cornucopia. The three symbols indicate the fauna, flora, and the minerals of Peru. The shield is placed on four flags of Peru.

The three libra denominations also feature the same designs on the obverse and reverse. The Indian head is the description used when mention is made of the obverse of the libra coins. The designer appeared to have had a Liberty head in mind when he designed the coin. The head appears to be a female with a band around her head with two feathers in the band. At any rate the face dominates the obverse of these three coins in the libra denominations.

The Spanish for "Truth and Justice" surround the head with the denomination under the design. The reverses of the three coins are similar and they display the coat-of-arms for Peru which was described above.

The sol was the unit selected by Peru in 1863 as a new monetary denomination; the Latin Monetary Union standards were then adopted. Various changes have been made since that time.

Peru has also introduced some 100- and 50-soles denominations in gold as commemorative coins. One of the more interesting was that produced for the 400th anniversary of the Lima Mint. The 100 soles carried the design on the obverse of the first coin of Peru—the 8 reales of 1565. The reverse carried the arms of Peru with denominations and the name of the Central Bank.

Another interesting gold coin was issued in 1966 for the centennial of the defeat of the Spanish fleet in the naval battle of 1866, a winged victory was the major design feature of the 100-soles coin.

The 50- and 100-soles commemoratives were struck to the same standards as the 50- and 100-soles listed above.

These gold coins with recent dates as well as the commemorative pieces with current dates are not considered to be coins in the true sense of the word.

The gold bullion pieces made in the likeness of coins are usually considered to be NCLT (Non-Circulating Legal Tender) and are usually cataloged as such in most coin catalogs or listings.

The NCLT does not reach out and get all of the gold bullion pieces as there are some that are not declared "legal tender" by the issuing country. The ducats of various countries are a couple of examples as well as the sovereigns of Great Britain.

The correct classification would be to call the pieces just what they are, gold bullion coins.

Gold bullion pieces float on the price of an ounce of gold; even in the likeness of coins—past or present—they still sell for the gold value and not collector value.

Peru has been a great producer of gold bullion pieces in the past years and their well-designed and well-struck gold bullion coins probably appeal to collectors as well as gold bullion purchasers or investors.

Russia

3 roubles 3.9 grams gross weight, .9166 gold fineness, 20 millimeters in diameter, 3.57 grams of gold or .1149 of an ounce of gold.

5 roubles 4.3 grams gross weight, .900 gold fineness, 18.5 millimeters in diameter, 3.87 grams of gold or .1244 of an ounce of gold.

7½ roubles 6.452 grams gross weight, .900 gold fineness, 21.5 millimeters in diameter, 5.80 grams of gold or .1866 of an ounce of gold.

10 roubles 8.602 grams gross weight, .900 gold fineness, 22.5 millimeters in
   diameter, 7.74 grams of gold or .2489 of an ounce of gold.
15 roubles 12.9 grams gross weight, .900 gold fineness, 24.5 millimeters in
   diameter, 11.61 grams of gold or .3732 of an ounce of gold.
1 chervonetz 8.60 grams gross weight, .900 gold fineness, 22.5 millimeters in
   diameter, 7.74 grams of gold or .2488 of an ounce of gold.

The coins of Russia can be divided into several sections, those of Imperial
Russia—ancient and modern—as well as those of the new Soviet Russia from
World War I to modern times.

Russian coinage in any material is difficult to trace as are their mintage
figures and types of issues they made.

In gold they have restruck almost every one of the older coins which would
cover a period of time from the year 1000 to the late 1800s. They have also
struck coin designs of other countries such as the Netherlands ducat of the
middle 1800s. Other pieces have been attributed to Russia as copies but collectors have not pinpointed most of the issues.

Restrikes from the mints in Russia are not a new fad or fancy. There are many
references to the restrikes or novodels for collectors in Russia as the pieces were
collected as carefully as the originals. It was quite normal to purchase restrikes,
made from the original dies, from the Russian mints. The habit started in the
time of Catherine the Great (1762–1796). Grand Duke George Mikhailovich who
did much for numismatists around the world when he cataloged Russian coins
did not like the idea.

Although gold bullion coins have little relationship with collector items it is
interesting to note that some gold bullion coins on the market may have old dates
because of restriking the pieces from old dies by the current mints.

In the time of Mikhailovich you could order complete collections of old coins
that had been out of circulation for some time. He wrote to the secretary of
finance about the problem and requested legislation which would put the
practice to an end. The date of his letter, 1891, was two hundred years after the
restrike program had been started. It is doubted if he had much influence as
World War I was just around the corner and Imperial Russia was about to end.

The coins listed in the above specifications are the most common ones to be
found in bullion or collector markets.

The 3-rouble gold coin was equal to the European ducat. From the middle
1800s the weight or gold fineness of the coin has not changed. The Russian issues
also conformed to the Latin Monetary Union.

The 5-rouble gold coin was minted with a heavier gross weight early in the
1800s as well as having a gold fineness of .9166. The initial weight was over 6.5
grams which was changed in 1886 to 6.4 grams and changed again in 1897 to
the lightweight 4.3 grams listed above.

The 7½-rouble gold coin took the place of the 5-rouble piece for purposes of the
Latin Monetary Union. The earlier issue of the 5 rouble was equal to 20 francs
and the 7½-rouble gold coin, after 1897, received the exchange value of 20 francs,
due to changes in the Latin Monetary Union.

The original 10-rouble gold coin, not listed above, was heavier in gross weight and gold weight. It first weighed over 12 grams but in 1898 it was changed to a lighter 8.6 grams coin. The exchange value in Latin Monetary Union francs was 40.

In 1897 the old 10-rouble gold coin was no longer equal to the Latin Monetary Union 40 francs so a new 15-rouble denomination was created to equal the new standards.

In 1923 a brand new gold issue was made by the Soviet Union called the chervonetz and this coin is a much wanted gold piece. It carries .2488 of an ounce of gold or 24 percent of an ounce and may be found on the gold bullion market. The 1923 date on the piece could be questioned as the pieces are probably newer than that date.

Russia, as well, is the second largest producer of gold next to South Africa and they have produced a great quantity of bullion coins for the world market.

One of the more interesting stories about Russian coinage is that of the platinum pieces that they made and tried to put into circulation in the early 1800s. At that time they first discovered platinum and used the material for coin issues. The grey color of the coin did not go well with the average Russian and the coins were rejected as circulation pieces.

In order to force the circulation of the platinum coins the Russians decided to gold plate the issues, which were then acceptable to the public. The gold-plated Russian platinum pieces are much sought after collector items.

After this operation had passed it was then determined that platinum was a very valuable material by world demand. Platinum passes the same chemical tests that gold is subjected to and it also has about the same density which makes a gold-plated platinum piece a difficult one to detect.

The last of the Czars was Nicholas II (1894–1917) and his coins have been produced in great quantities, at the time and by Middle East counterfeiters. They are on the gold bullion market. Any date in his reign can be found, which may or may not be on genuine pieces.

The gold content in most of the counterfeit gold coins is up to original specifications. The striking of gold coins for smuggling purposes is quite common in the Middle East as the coins are easier to handle. Small gold bars would be more of a hazard to smuggle but more gold can be carried in bar form.

The gold content of the fake Nicholas II has been normally found to be quite authentic and those coins of the 5- and 10-rouble denominations are often bought and sold on the gold bullion market, everywhere in the world.

Many of the earlier gold coins of the 1800s, those issued under Alexander III (1881–1894) did not have the portrait of Alexander. They carried the Russian arms on one side of the coin and the weight on the other face. Upon return to the portrait types on the gold issues the head is surrounded by the Cyrillic inscription which gives the titles of the ruler with the reverse showing the Russian arms, the imperial arms, and not the current U.S.S.R. design.

The imperial coat-of-arms carried the double-headed eagle, a device that dates back to at least 1100, and maybe further back in time, to Frederick Barbarossa who was elected King of the Romans in 1152 and crowned as emperor in 1155. As head of the Holy Roman Empire he appears to have used the first double-eagle design to denote the office.

There are students of the heraldic designs who have insisted that the double-headed eagle was not designed as one body with two heads. They point to the fact that it is two eagles, one over the other, with their heads facing in different directions. As the bird represented the Holy Roman Empire when it was divided into East and West so the heads point in those directions.

The controversy will probably never cease in regard to the double-headed eagle design and which finally evolved as the emblem of the Holy Roman Empire as well as an imperial emblem.

The orb held by the eagle in the arms represents the world as it did in ancient Roman times and it is held in the sinister claw of the bird. The sceptre is held in the dexter claw. On the wings of the eagle are the shields which show the arms of other states.

The small arms shown on the right wing of the eagle represent Finland, Siberia, Astrakan, and Caucasus. On the left wing can be found the arms of Poland, Chersonese Taurida, Kasan, Kiev Novgorod Waladimir. On the breast of the eagle is St. George slaying the dragon, a favorite design in Russia which dates back many years to their ancient history.

The denomination of the coin, date, and mint mark appear under this design all of which are on the reverse of the coin.

The modern issue in 1923 of the 1 chervonetz or 10 roubles is not linked in any way with the issues of chervonetz minted in the 1700s without denominations. The 1700 issues were also considered to be ducat denominations, either a 1- or 2-ducat denomination depending upon their diameter.

To gold bullion investors the important question is not about mint marks, dates, or inscriptions but is about the authenticity of the amount of gold in the piece.

South Africa

1 rand   3.99 grams gross weight, .9166 gold fineness, 19 millimeters in diameter, 3.66 grams of gold or .11771 of an ounce of gold.

2 rand   7.98 grams gross weight, .9166 gold fineness, 22 millimeters in diameter, 7.322 grams of gold or .23542 of an ounce of gold.

Krugerrand   33.93 grams gross weight, .9166 gold fineness, 32.69 millimeters in diameter, 31.1035 grams of gold or 1 troy ounce.

The Krugerrand gold piece from South Africa has completely changed the investment scene in respect to the holding of gold.

Two dramatic happenings have occurred to gold in the past few years. One was the export from South Africa of the Krugerrand while the other was the elimination of all of the gold regulations of the United States.

The Krugerrand was first *exported* in 1970 from South Africa to the rest of the world that allowed their citizens to hold gold which at the time did not include the United States.

On December 31, 1974, Public Law 93-373 of the United States terminated all legal prohibitions on United States citizens purchasing, holding, selling, or otherwise dealing in gold.

Those two events caused a great change in the ideas about gold to the average citizen. To collectors of gold coins the law was a welcome change from previous bureaucratic regulations.

Another boost in the gold product of South Africa, as well as being a direct benefit of all gold bullion coins, was the marketing idea from the International Gold Corporation Limited, the promotion source of the Chamber of Mines in South Africa. They announced a $4,000,000 advertising campaign which was started in the fall of 1976.

The American advertising agency prepared the campaign which was directed at 25 major United States markets.

The theme of the promotion was "the world's best way of owning pure gold." There is no question about the end result of the campaign. It not only produced new and higher sales for the Krugerrand but also increased interest in every form of gold bullion presented on the commodity market.

Prior to the campaign it is questionable if any persons outside of the numismatic field recognized the name of Krugerrand. Today the gold bullion coin is known by almost everyone everywhere.

The simple idea of making a gold bullion piece which carries an ounce of gold based on the latest daily gold quotes also helped sell the Krugerrand.

The Krugerrand receives its name from both a man and an area. The man was Stephanus Johanus Paulus Kruger. Born in 1825, he eventually became a South African statesman who migrated in the "Great Trek" of 1836–1840 and founded the Transvaal State. He was a leader in the Boer revolution and later aided in negotiating a peace treaty. Kruger was president of the Transvaal from 1893 to 1900. He died in Switzerland in 1904.

The area called the Rand is the shortest name for Witwatersrand (ridge of white waters), the area in Transvaal with the great gold deposits.

The Krugerrand carries the portrait of Paul Kruger on the obverse taken from earlier portraits found on the coinage of the Zuid-Afrikaansche Republiek issued while Kruger was president. The gold pieces issued in his administration were the ½ and 1 pond which today are valued as collector items and not gold bullion coins.

The reverse design of the famed Krugerrand is the image of the Springbok the name of the animal in Afrikaans, Sprinbuck in English, and *Antidorcas marsupialis* in scholarly language. This small African gazelle is noted for sudden leaps into the air and most stand less than a yard high at shoulder height.

With the current fluctuation of the price of gold, per ounce, the Springbok is certainly an apropos design to have on this world-famed gold bullion coin, as gold has certainly leaped suddenly into the air.

The reverse wording is in Afrikaans and English stating "Fyngoud 1 oz. fine gold."

Checking with various dealers that sell the South African Krugerrand it is found that very few of the purchasers are collecting year dates of the issue, as most sales are mainly for the gold bullion value of the piece.

There are collector coins made each year for collectors of the Krugerrand. Those issues are made in the proof process, the ultimate in coin production with special dies, polished blanks, and careful handling of the pieces. These proofs are made in a limited production quantity and sold for a premium over the bullion Krugerrand. The percentage over the bullion value may be as high as 50 percent.

As an example of the small production of the proof Krugerrands it should be noted that in 1978 South Africa produced 6,106,980 Krugerrands for gold bullion world sales but only minted 10,000 of the proof Krugerrands in the same year.

Two other gold coins were also minted in limited quantities in 1978. One was a commemorative for the leader of the first Dutch colony that settled in the Cape of Good Hope in 1652, Jan van Riebeeck. That issue totaled about 30,000 coins with 19,000 of them produced by the proof process. It was a 2-rand denomination made from 91.6 percent fine gold with a gold ounce content of .2354.

The second gold commemorative coin was a 1 rand minted in commemoration of the same event but in a smaller denomination and with less gold content. This coin carries only 11 percent of an ounce of gold. The mintage was a little over 50,000 pieces with 19,000 of them as proof coins.

The 2-rand piece was introduced into the United States in late 1979. The 1 rand was waiting to see how well its larger cousin was received before coming to America.

All of the South African coin production is made by the South African Mint in Pretoria. At the time that President Paul Kruger was in office the initial coins for use in the Transvaal were made by the Prussian Mint in Berlin, Germany.

Already mentioned was the gold pond denominations but a series of bronze and silver coins was also struck. The 5-shilling silver coin and the pond gold coins were initially produced with a mistake in the design of the wagon shown on the reverse of the coins as part of the overall design.

The wagon design with two shafts attached to the pulling animal was incorrect as the wagons used on The Great Trek by the Voortrekkers were one-shaft wagons. The other error in the design originally found on the coin was the fact that the wagons were shown with wheels of the same diameter. The wagons actually used different-sized wheels on the front and back.

Probably the last bit of irony to the design was the addition of the initials of the designer, Otto Schultz, under the portrait of President Kruger. The OS being noted as ox in Afrikaans. Corrections were made in the dies and both varieties are listed in numismatic catalogs as "single shaft" or "double shaft" coins.

The Pretoria Mint was opened as a branch of the Royal Mint after the Boer War and in the formation of the Union of South Africa in 1910.

The minting of gold coins at that time were the British sovereign and half sovereign with the SA mint mark of South Africa which lasted until 1932.

Gold coins were again struck in the 1950s but still on the British system which was retained until South Africa became an independent republic in 1961.

The new Republic of South Africa then went on the decimal system and started striking the 1- and 2-rand denominations in gold. By 1977 the 1-rand coin used for general circulation had been reduced to copper-nickel.

Only the commemorative gold coins retained the tradition of gold for the 1- and 2-rand denominations.

(The language, Afrikaans, is a Dutch dialect as the Dutch were the first to land in the area and they left their stamp on the language of South Africa. In fact the dual languages of Afrikaans and English are used on the coinage of South Africa.)

The Krugerrand was first introduced in 1967 and collectors have been on the trail of the golden ounce since that time. In 1970 the Krugerrands were first exported and production of the coin has increased at least three times over the original mintage figures.

The sale of the 1-ounce gold coin is accomplished in a series of distribution steps. The first step is the distribution by the gold-selling organization of the South African Chamber of Mines, the International Gold Corporation. They distribute Krugerrands through exclusive contracts with distributors in each country.

The distributors then sell the pieces to other selected brokers and dealers normally in lots of not less than 250 coins.

This group then breaks down the 250-coin lots to 10- or 50-lot sizes and sells the pieces to the smaller banks and coin dealers in the country. This is then the retail market for the coins which are sold to consumers.

Each in turn takes a small premium for the handling of the product which the consumer purchases at a percentage over the gold bullion value of the coin (see Chapter 1).

Spain

10 pesetas 3.225 grams gross weight, .900 gold fineness, 19 millimeters in diameter, 2.90 grams of gold or .0933 of an ounce of gold.

25 pesetas 8.06 grams gross weight, .900 gold fineness, 24 millimeters in diameter, 7.25 grams of gold or .2332 of an ounce of gold.

The above have the image of Alfonso XII.

20 pesetas 6.45 grams gross weight, .900 gold fineness, 21 millimeters in diameter, 5.80 grams of gold or .1866 of an ounce of gold.

100 pesetas 32.258 grams gross weight, .900 gold fineness, 35 millimeters in diameter, 29.03 grams of gold or .9334 of an ounce of gold.

The above have the image of Alfonso XIII.

The last Spanish coins issued were those of Alfonso XII and Alfonso XIII with the last issue dated 1904. Official restrikes have been made of the issues of the two mentioned rulers and they carry the date of original issue as designed but also carry the restrike date divided into two figures in stars which flank the large date.

The designs of the gold coins from Spain are the same for all issues with the exception of the different ages of the heads of state which are represented.

The 10- and 20-pesetas gold coins with the image of Alfonso XII were originally issued in the 1876–1880 era. In each case the young head of the king was used as he reigned from 1874 to 1885. Actually the older head used on the issues of 1881 (which have not been restruck to our knowledge) really is only a bearded king.

The obverse of the coins (10 and 20 pesetas) carries the information that

Alfonso XII was "by the grace of God [continued on the reverse] Constitutional King of Spain." The reverse design is the arms of Spain.

The large date on the obverse indicates the date of the original issue while the small stars that flank the date will reveal the year of striking.

The arms of Spain displayed on all of the gold issues under question as gold bullion pieces is a complicated design.

The arms described was first introduced in 1938 but the design has had centuries of putting together all of the pieces of the puzzle.

The actual kingdom of Spain did not exist until 1492 when the fall of Granada made Isabella I and Ferdinand V rulers of the whole land of Spain. Prior to that time the country was ruled in bits and pieces until unified areas such as Aragon joined with Barcelona in 1137, Castile with Leon in 1230, and joined the other two in 1479.

The coat-of-arms seen on the coins then has a number of quarterings for the above mentioned places. Castile is represented by a castle, Leon by a lion, Aragon by red stripes on a yellow background, Navarre by chains, and Granada by the pomegranate, all of which date back to 1500. The big eagle came from the old Roman symbol which is flanked by the Pillars of Hercules and crowned by the imperial and royal crowns. The yoke and arrows under the eagle are old Spanish symbols and were the badges of Isabella and Ferdinand. The motto on the pillars is "Plvs Vltra" or there is "more beyond," in reference to the world beyond the Straits of Gibraltar.

The flag of Spain is a middle gold stripe with a red stripe above and below with the emblem described in the center of the gold stripe. That was adopted in the period following the Spanish civil war in the 1930s.

Switzerland

10 francs 3.225 grams gross weight, .900 gold fineness, 19 millimeters in diameter, 2.90 grams of gold or .0933 of an ounce of gold.

20 francs 6.452 grams gross weight, .900 gold fineness, 21 millimeters in diameter, 5.806 grams of gold or .1867 of an ounce of gold.

100 francs 32.288 grams gross weight, .900 gold fineness, 35 millimeters in diameter, 29.05 grams of gold or .9342 of an ounce of gold.

The most common gold coins from Switzerland are the 10- and 20-franc pieces with the 20-franc coins being the most abundant. The 100-franc denomination was used as a reference coin, in the above listing, to indicate the size of the larger 100-franc pieces produced in the early 1920s. The current 100-franc coins from Switzerland are smaller in diameter (26 millimeters) with only 17.5 grams gross weight with .900 fine gold, which makes the piece contain only 50 percent of an ounce of gold compared to the 93 percent of the listed coin.

Most of the gold coins of Switzerland have an edge design of 22 stars which represent the 22 cantons of the country.

Under the law of 1931 new 20-franc coins were produced with the edge stating in Latin "under the law of 1931." There is a lot of confusion about the marking on the 20 franc issued in 1939, 1947, and 1949.

In 1935 they produced a great quantity of 20-franc gold coins according to mintage figures. The real truth of the matter is the fact that only a small quantity of 20-franc pieces were minted in 1935. The majority of the 1935 dated production of 20-franc pieces took place in 1945, 1946, and 1948. This production is indicated by a small "L" to the left of the date and the pieces display the 22 stars on the edge or rim of the coin.

In 1947 and 1948 they also struck 20-franc gold coins with those dates. The small "L" was not placed on the left side of the date and the edge or rim does not carry 22 stars. The wording of "Ad Legem Anni MCMXXXI" is found on the rim and only 7 stars appear. The wording simply states, "under the law of 1931."

The 20-franc coin carried the head of a girl against the background of the Swiss Alps with the "Helvetia" for Switzerland around the top of the design. The reverse carries the simple arms of Switzerland.

The common 10-franc gold coin encountered is one with the same obverse design but the reverse is different. Instead of the arms of Switzerland it has a radiant cross at the top with denomination in the center of the coin and date underneath with a floral design in exergue. The 100-franc coin specified above has the same design with the exception of the denomination.

The coat-of-arms for Switzerland described by law in 1814 and again in 1941 is a white cross on a red background—a known symbol for freedom since the 14th century.

Switzerland has four official languages: German, French, Italian, and Romansh. There are twenty-five federated states which consist of nineteen cantons and six half-cantons for a total of twenty-two cantons. The Swiss Federation was first formed in 1291 and the various cantons and half-cantons joined from that time until the last three united in 1815.

Their flag—the white cross on a red background—was adopted in 1848 but the actual cross with the four equal arms is more modern than that date.

The adoption of a Federal Constitution in 1848 stopped the practice of each of the cantons issuing their own gold coins.

Turkey

25 piastres 1.804 grams gross weight, .9166 gold fineness, 14.5 millimeters for standard, 18 millimeters for deluxe, 1.653 grams of gold or .0531 of an ounce of gold.

50 piastres 3.608 grams gross weight, .9166 gold fineness, 18 millimeters for standard, 22 millimeters for deluxe, 3.307 grams of gold or .1063 of an ounce of gold.

100 piastres 7.216 grams gross weight, .9166 gold fineness, 22 millimeters for standard, 30 millimeters for deluxe, 6.614 grams of gold or .2126 of an ounce of gold.

250 piastres 18.04 grams gross weight, .9166 gold fineness, 27 millimeters for standard, 40 millimeters for deluxe, 16.535 grams of gold or .5316 of an ounce of gold.

500 piastres 36.08 grams gross weight, .9166 gold fineness, 35 millimeters for standard, 45 millimeters for deluxe, 33.07 grams of gold or 1.063 ounces of gold.

The descriptions above include the diameters of the standard gold coins as well as the deluxe for each denomination. In any given denomination the gold content is the same as is the gross weight but the deluxe coins are thinner and have an ornate border which gives them a larger diameter. This practice for gold coins in Turkey has been in vogue since 1876.

That double issue as well as a great number of denominations has to rank Turkey as one of the greatest gold coin producing nations. The inability of most persons to read the Turkish language has caused most collectors to shy away from an interesting series of gold coins.

Under the Sultans they issued uniform pattern pieces but changes in the legends for each Sultan and design changes made a wide variety of coins.

Confusion is also a good word to describe the modern issues of Turkey for several reasons.

One of the reasons is the fact that they still strike coins for former President Kemal Ataturk who was the first president of the Turkish Republic in 1923 and lasted until his death in 1938. Turkey issues coins to this day in his honor. All have the date of 1923 with a second digit under the date which added to the 1923 date gives the actual year of issue. This minting started in 1943.

The coins do not have a denomination but are determined by size in both the standard and deluxe issues.

At the same time, they issued a similar series of gold coins for the next president, Ismet Inonu (1938–1950). There is no information about striking coins for the current president.

On the standard coin issues the obverse legend is normally "Sovereignty is of the people." The name of the striking mint is usually below the portrait. On the reverse of the gold standard coins is "Turkish Republic." On the money deluxe the legend is not on the obverse but is on the reverse with the date in the Turkish language.

It is unknown as to the number or types of Turkish coins that are involved in the gold bullion market, but the ones listed are involved as official issues. Without denomination or indication of fineness of the gold in the coins it is difficult to quickly identify the gold pieces with the single exception of knowing the difference between a standard and deluxe issue.

United States

$1   1.6718 grams gross weight, .900 gold fineness, 15 millimeters in diameter, 1.50 grams of gold or .0483 of an ounce of gold.

$2.50 *Quarter Eagle*   4.18 grams gross weight, .900 gold fineness, 18 millimeters in diameter, 3.762 grams of gold or .1209 of an ounce of gold.

$3   5.015 grams gross weight, .900 gold fineness, 20.5 millimeters in diameter, 4.513 grams of gold or .1451 of an ounce of gold.

$5 *Half Eagle*   8.359 grams gross weight, .900 gold fineness, 21.6 millimeters in diameter, 7.523 grams of gold or .2418 of an ounce of gold.

$10 Eagle 16.718 grams gross weight, .900 gold fineness, 27 millimeters in diameter, 15.04 grams of gold or .4837 of an ounce of gold.

$20 Double Eagle 33.436 grams gross weight, .900 gold fineness, 34 millimeters in diameter, 30.09 grams of gold or .9674 of an ounce of gold.

The gold coins of the United States never really entered the gold bullion classification until the price of gold reached over $400 an ounce. Then some of the common-dated gold pieces were sold by their owners for the gold bullion price and not the collector value. Most of the gold coins of the U.S. are valued at a premium over bullion value due to collector demand for the coins.

The specifications given are those for the last issues of the denominations listed. There are variations in sizes and weights from earlier-dated coins but many U.S. coin guides can produce that information, as well as information about mint marks, grading conditions, and other numismatic information (see Chapter 7).

United States coin collectors have made a specialty of collecting gold coins by date as well as mint mark and this has produced high values for limited editions from mints which were in operation a short time.

The $1 gold coin was minted for a short time, in relation to other denominations, from 1849 through 1889. Some of the earlier issues were minted in the Charlotte, North Carolina mint (C mint mark) which minted only gold coins from 1838 to 1861. The D mint mark of Dahlonega, Georgia also can be found on certain issues of the gold dollar as can the O of New Orleans. The normal average coin will probably be one minted in Philadelphia and those have no mint marks. The mint mark if on the coin is found under the wreath on the reverse of the coin.

The $2.50 or quarter eagle was minted from 1796 to 1929. Being struck for that length of time did not insure that every mint would make the coin. Carson City with its CC mint mark missed out on making the coin. The $2.50 gold coin underwent several changes of design in the span in which it was made. One of the most important took place in 1908 when it was changed to a Bela Lyon Pratt design which was incused on the coin. This is the opposite of the normal coin with the raised design. The immediate effect by many was criticism of the design because it would cause the coins to collect dirt in the sunken design. The piece survived from 1908 to 1929.

The $3 gold coin of the United States was another denomination that was not imitated in the U.S. paper money series; the other coin was the $2.50 gold piece, the oddity being the fact that the denominations were used as coins but not on notes.

The $3 gold coin was minted from 1854 through 1889. The mint mark, if any, appears on the reverse under the wreath. Most of the production was made in the Philadelphia Mint for the years it existed. Normally this denomination is not considered to be a gold bullion coin as its value is greater than the gold bullion value. Few if any would be sold as a non-collectors coin.

The $5 coin or the half eagle is the one coin that is sought after if a collector ever takes the trail of mint marks. The $5 gold coin was the only denomination in the gold series to be struck at every one of the seven mint facilities.

It is also a good gold bullion coin because some of the common mintages have values at or a little above the gold ounce price. There were several design changes in the years it was minted starting in 1795 and ending in 1929.

The last issue of the half eagle from 1908 to 1929 was of the same design as the quarter eagle with the incused design. The coin received the same criticism as did the $2.50 gold piece.

The eagle or $10 gold coin was minted from 1795 to 1933 but not all of the mints struck the coin. It also underwent several design changes in its lifetime as well as changing in size from the original 33 millimeters to its final size of 27 millimeters in diameter. Some of the more common dates, which would indicate a large mintage, might be priced in the gold bullion range. That would also depend upon the price of an ounce of gold on the commodity markets. When gold broke over the $420 to $430 mark many of the common dates were sold. Normally the price of a $10 gold coin is almost a hundred dollars higher than the gold ounce price for the coin.

The $20 gold coin called the double eagle is a much wanted gold coin. As with all United States gold coins the face value of the coin was equal to the gold value in the coin when struck.

The $20 gold coin had $20 worth of gold when gold was valued at $20.67 an ounce which gives it 96 percent of an ounce of gold.

DELEGALIZATION OF U.S. GOLD

On March 6, 1933, President Roosevelt proclaimed the bank holiday and all gold was put under license for the holiday period. Three days later, March 9, 1933, there was a Congressional Act that required the people to deliver their gold to the United States Treasury. On the following day, March 10, 1933, the exportation of gold was prohibited except as authorized by the Secretary of the Treasury under the license requirement of March 6.

On April 5, 1933, President Roosevelt issued Executive Order No. 6102 requiring delivery of all gold coins to the United States with the exception of gold and gold certificates not exceeding in the aggregate $100 and gold coin having a recognized special value to collectors of rare and unusual coins.

The above Executive Order reads quite well today, but at the time it was issued a great number of the officials could not determine the "rare and unusual" gold coins. Many of the common dates went to the government from the hands of collectors. It may not have been intended that way but that is what happened. At $20 per ounce all gold was confiscated from the public and melted into ingot form.

On May 12, 1933, provision was made for fiat money, devaluation of the dollar, as well as other devaluation measures. All new money was declared to be full legal tender for all debts. Reduction of the weight of gold and silver dollars was made by proclamation but it could not be reduced more than 50 percent.

All contracts with gold clauses were abolished and declared to be against the public policy. This was approved on June 10, 1933.

Things with gold weren't going so well—as the public seemed to be dragging their feet on the matter as late as July and August of 1933. This caused another order to the public to give up their gold, dated August 28, 1933. Again the permission to have gold of recognized value was stated—but softly.

At this time it is interesting to note that President Roosevelt declared that he had taken the U.S. off the gold standard and started the country in the direction of currency inflation. The idea, at that time in 1933, was to raise domestic prices to the 1926 level and then stop at that point.

On August 29, 1933, the regulation of gold to the arts and industry began.

On January 30, 1934, the Gold Reserve Act of 1934 was approved by Roosevelt and the next day the gold dollar was devalued about 41 percent.

The United States at that time made the turn at the corner of currency debasement by the confiscation of public held gold in return for paper money which has the clause, "promise to pay."

President Roosevelt in 1933–1934 fixed the official price of gold at $35 per ounce which was raised from the old $20.67 per ounce price. Roosevelt stated that he took the action in order to start inflation.

In the term of President Nixon gold prices were officially raised from $35 per ounce to $38 per ounce and then again to $42.22 per ounce on October 9, 1973.

Digging back into dusty archives it was discovered that in the middle of 1933 it was estimated that more than $600 million in gold was still hiding. Secretary of the Treasury Woodin had a list of names compiled of those who might have gold hoards. They queried about 1,840 persons and found that 95, with gold hoards which amounted to several hundred thousand dollars, flatly refused to obey the gold turn-in order.

The administration invoked fines and jail sentences for some in order to get the rest in line with the policy.

This kind of publicity caused a number of those with rare or uncommon coins to turn in those gold pieces. Many a collector turned in gold coins due to the gold orders which had received the most newsprint.

The Gold Regulations of the U.S. Treasury were produced due to the Gold Reserve Act of 1934.

The many revisions to the Gold Regulations made them "livable but laughable" according to those who had to use the regulations. Many of the paragraphs were obsolete but they were also hard to change or revise without a long time between acts.

Finally on December 31, 1974, the Gold Regulations were removed and went into history.

"Public Law 93-373 terminated all legal prohibitions on U.S. citizens purchasing, holding, selling or otherwise dealing in gold, effective December 31, 1974. To reflect the effect of the law, the Treasury Department Gold Regulations and licensing procedures have been revoked." That was the last word received from the U.S. Treasury on the subject.

A NEW U.S. GOLD COIN?

Prior to the great surge of interest in gold and the corresponding price rise that occurred in 1979, the U.S. Treasury announced its intentions of minting its own gold pieces.

Congress has yet to appropriate the necessary funds to start the project but in case they do the U.S. Mint will produce 1-ounce and ½-ounce gold pieces which have been tentatively called "gold medallions," nomenclature which is incorrect for the type of item to be produced.

The Congress first authorized the American Arts Gold Medallion Act on November 10, 1978. At that time it was determined that the ounce and ½-ounce pieces would be produced as a series of gold pieces, to be made over a span of five years.

The selections of the first ten designs to be used have already been made. The 1 ounce would have Grant Wood on the first issue and Marian Anderson on the first ½-ounce gold piece. The second year issues would not be made until success or failure had been determined by the first year sales.

The second year designs would then be Mark Twain on the 1-ounce piece and Willa Cather on the ½-ounce piece. In the third year the sculptor Alexander Calder is destined to be on the ½ ounce while poet Robert Frost would be the object of the 1-ounce gold piece.

Architect Frank Lloyd Wright is planned for the ½-ounce piece for the fourth year with the 1 ounce showing Louis Armstrong. For the fifth and final year the ½ ounce will have John Steinbeck and the 1 ounce will carry Helen Hayes.

These medals were originally planned to be sold to the public at a premium over the free market value of an ounce of gold at the time of sale.

This idea is to get around the U.S. Treasury objections to selling ½- and 1-ounce gold pieces to the U.S. public. It is more interested in selling large quantities of gold at auction, rather than the small weights individually.

The gold material will come from Treasury stockpiles or surplus which mainly came from the gold coins taken from the public in 1933 at $20.67 per ounce.

There is talk of a gold coin similar to the Krugerrand being produced and sold by the United States but so far action on the idea has not reached any level of excitement.

Index

A

Albert, King of Belgium, 96
Alexander III, Czar of Russia, 117
Alfonso XII, King of Spain, 121–22
Alfonso XIII, King of Spain, 121
American Arts Gold Medallion Act (1978), 128
American Numismatic Association, 89, 91
Anderson, Marian, 128
Apulia, Duke of (Austria), 94
Armstrong, Louis, 128
Assay, definition of, 3
Ataturk, President Kemal (Turkey), 124
Australia
  discovery of gold in, 17–18
  gold mining industry in, 41

Austria, coins of, 5, 9, 11, 12, 93–95
Avoirdupois system of measurement (U.S.), 14

B

Bailey, Clement F., 93
Banks, as source for gold purchase, 2, 12, 26
Banu, Arjumand, 109
Barbarossa, Frederick, King of the Romans, 117
Beauty, as reason for buying gold, xi, xii–xvi
Belgium, coins of, 95–96
Blocked money, 22
Bolivar, Simon, 99
Bowers, Q. David, 91

129

Homestake mine (South Dakota),
17
Hungary, coins of, 5, 9, 11, 12,
105-7

I

IMF (International Monetary
Fund), 22, 27, 45, 49
IMM (International Monetary
Market), 72, 81
India, coins of, 107-9
Inflation, 40, 46-47, 55
Ingot(s), 4, 11-12, 26. *See also*
Gold bars
Inonu, President Ismet (Turkey),
124
Insurance on gold bullion
investment, 67
International Financial Statistics,
61
International Gold Corporation,
121
International Monetary Fund
(IMF)
creation of, 45, 49
role of, in sale of gold, 22, 27
International Monetary Market
(IMM) of the Chicago
Mercantile Exchange, 72, 81
Investment (gold)
and the costs of purchase, 67
as important to supply/demand
ratio, 33, 35
how to make, 1-14
making a profit on, 62-70
and playing the field, 64-66
and price patterns, 68-70
and the psychological price
barrier, 67-68
reasons for, xi, xix-xxi
and the use of borrowed money,
66-67

and the use of strategy in, 62,
63-64
and the use of technical
analysis, 67
Investors as purchasers of gold,
35-36
Isabella I, Queen of Spain, 122
Italy, gold holdings of, 51

J

Jahan, Shah, 109
Jefferson Nickel (U. S.), 86
Jewelry (gold)
mark-up in price of, xiv
as often poor investment,
xii-xvi, 2-3
value of, 83
John II, Prince of Liechtenstein,
110
Johnson, Matthey, Ltd., 25
Joseph John Adam, Prince of
Liechtenstein, 109, 110
Joseph Wenzel, Prince of
Liechtenstein, 109

K

Karat, xv, 3
Karl I, Emperor of Austria, 95
Kennecott copper mine (Utah), 17
Kennedy Half Dollar (U.S.), 86, 87
Klerksdrop area (South Africa),
20
Klondike gold rush, 18
Kopeck (Russia), 22
Korona (Hungary), 105
Krahmann, Rudolph, 19
Kruger, Stephanus Johanus
Paulus, 18, 119, 120
Krugerrand (South Africa), 5-6,
7, 8, 12, 29, 112, 118-21

L

Latin Monetary Union, 94, 106, 115, 116–17
Leopold I, King of Belgium, 96
Libra (Peru), 113–15
Liechtenstein, coins of, 109–10
Lincoln Cent (U.S.), 86
London free gold market, 47
London gold fixing, 25
Long position in gold futures, 79

M

Mahall, Mumtaz, 109
Maintenance margin, 77
Maple Leaf (Canada), 5, 8, 10, 12, 96
Margin call, 77
Marshall Plan, 45
Mercury Dime (U.S.), 86
Mexico
   coins of, 5, 9, 11, 12, 110–13
   gold as found in, 23
Mikhailovich, Grand Duke George (Russia), 116
Mint condition, 89
Mint state, 89
Mintage of U.S. coins, 42, 87–88, 125
Mocatta and Goldsmid, 25
Mohur (India), 107, 108
Montagu, Samuel and Co., Ltd., 25
Morgan Dollar (U.S.), 86
Mystique, as reason for buying gold, xi, xvii–xix

N

National Commemorative Society, 102
NCLT (Non-Circulating Legal Tender), 115
Netherlands, coins of, 113

Netherlands East Indies, coins of, 113
New gold, 26
New Orleans (Louisiana) mint, 125
New York Mercantile Exchange, 72, 81
Nicholas II, Czar of Russia, 117
Nixon, Richard, 49, 127
Numismatic gold, 12, 82–83. See also Bullion coins
   condition of, 89–90
   mintage of, 87–88
   scarcity of, 87
Numismatic value, 82–83

O

"Official ANA Grading Standards for U.S. Coins," 89
Old gold, 27
Ooshuizen farm (South Africa), 18
OPEC oil cartel, effect of, on U.S. dollar, 53, 55, 58
Orange Free State Field (South Africa), 20

P

Panning for gold, 16
Paper currency
   increasing issuance of, following depression, 43
   as backed by silver or gold, xviii, 40
Paper gold, 49
Peace Dollar (U.S.), 86
Peru
   coins of, 113–15
   gold as found in, 23
Peseta (Spain), 121
Peso (Chile), 98
Peso (Columbia), 98

Sovereign (India), 107, 108
Soviet Union. *See* Russia
Spain, coins of, 121–22
Special Drawing Rights (SDR), 49
Speculators and gold futures,
    78–81
Spot price, definition of, 75
Steinbeck, John, 128
Sutro, Adolph, 17
Swiss Bank Corporation, 26
Swiss banking laws, and the
    supply/demand of gold, 26
Swiss Credit Bank, 12, 26
Swiss Franc standard, 110
Switzerland, coins of, 122–23
Substitution and the law of
    supply/demand, 30–31

T

Tips, as bad basis for investing in
    gold, 64
Troy system of measurement, 14
Turkey, coins of, 123–24
Twain, Mark, 128

U

Union Bank of Switzerland, 26
United States
    coins of, 13, 41, 42, 83, 84–85,
        86, 87, 124–28
    currency of, as backed by
        government, xviii, 40
    delegalization of gold in, 48, 88
    and the gold standard, 39–49
    intervention of, into gold
        market, 59–61
    legalization of gold in, 50–51
    as a major source of stored gold,
        27

and the minting of a new coin,
    127–28
non-gold policy of, 49–50
repurchase of gold by, 54
and the selling of gold reserves
    by, 27, 35, 36, 38
Unity coin (Canada), 97
U.S. dollar
    devaluation of, 49, 54
    stability of, 45–47
U.S. Mint, 101, 128
U.S. Office of Gold and Silver
    Operations, 107
Users, as purchasers of gold, 35

V

VDB Cent (U.S.), 86
Vereinstaler (Liechtenstein), 109
Victoria, Queen of England, 104,
    105, 108
Vietnam War, effect of, on U.S.
    dollar, 53

W

Wall Street Journal, The, 60
Washington Quarter (U.S.), 86
Western reserves of gold, 25, 33
William IV, King of England, 107
Wood, Grant, 128
Woodin, William H., 127
Wright, Frank Lloyd, 128

Y–Z

Yeoman, R. S., 87
Yukon territory, discovery of gold
    in, 18
Zurich (Switzerland), as biggest
    gold market, 25–26